WITHDRAWN

Pennsylvania & *the*
War of 1812

Pennsylvania

& the

War of 1812

Victor A. Sapio

The UNIVERSITY PRESS
of KENTUCKY

Standard Book No. 8131-1193-5
Library of Congress Catalog
Card No. 70-94070

*Serving Berea College, Centre College of Kentucky, Eastern
Kentucky University, Kentucky State College, Morehead State
University, Murray State University, University of Kentucky,
University of Louisville, and Western Kentucky University.*

To
  Baby

Contents

Acknowledgments

I wish to thank Dr. David Sterling who suggested the topic and Dr. Harry Coles who directed my first studies in this field. His guidance prevented many errors while his enthusiasm and encouragement revived my often flagging spirits. Drs. Clayton Roberts and Eugene Roseboom read the first draft of the manuscript and made valuable suggestions.

The staffs of the Library of Congress, the Historical Society of Pennsylvania, the Western Pennsylvania Historical Society, and the Carnegie Library of Pittsburgh were always cooperative and directed me to many sources I would otherwise have missed. I wish particularly to thank Miss Bayley Ellen Marks and Miss Ellen Lee Barker of the Maryland Historical Society for their assistance.

My colleagues at Colorado State University—Carlos Allen, John Jenkins, William Griswold, and Arnold Blumberg, and Joseph Cox at Towson State College always gave their time and knowledge when I requested it. Mrs. Irene Maddox typed various drafts of the manuscript with unfailing care.

To Mrs. Rudolph Wendel I owe a personal debt I can never repay. My dedication of this book to her is intended only to express my appreciation of that indebtedness.

Finally, I must thank my wife, Barbara Tooley Sapio. She supported me through graduate school and generously provided freedom from family responsibilities to give me time to do research and write.

V. A. S.

Introduction

The causes of the War of 1812 have produced a historiographical controversy far out of proportion to the war's military importance. The major reason for the debate is that the explanations of contemporary historians have proved inconsistent and unsatisfactory.[1] Those who had participated in the war in a military or political capacity generally agreed that the United States went to war to protect its maritime commerce and neutral rights against the predatory policies of Great Britain—policies which not only destroyed United States commerce, but insulted national honor and threatened the country's international prestige.[2] Historians, in the late nineteenth century, although on occasion intimating that other factors may also have played a role, accepted this maritime interpretation.[3]

Early in the twentieth century, historians looking at the distribution of the congressional vote for war began to have doubts about the validity of the maritime interpretation. They were impressed by the strong support in the Mississippi Valley and the opposition of the Northeast. A war supported by the West, the nation's noncommercial area, and fanatically opposed by New England, the nation's commercial center, could not have been fought exclusively for the protection of seamen's rights and commerce.[4]

Soon numerous monographs and books appeared which attempted to analyze other factors which might have prompted the nation to go to war. Most of these tried to explain the West's support. Land hunger, fear of a British-supported Indian uprising, economic depression, and an exuberance of youthful patriotism were advanced as possible causes.[5] When it was pointed out that the West, however valid its reasons, and however strong its support for the war, had neither the votes nor the influence

[1] Reginald Horsman, "Western War Aims, 1811-1812," *Indiana Magazine of History*, LIII (January, 1957), 1-18. For an excellent survey of the historiographical controversy to 1942 see Warren H. Goodman, "The Origins of the War of 1812: A Survey of Changing Interpretations," *Mississippi Valley Historical Review*, XXVIII (September, 1941), 171-87.

[2] H. M. Brackenridge, *History of the Late War Between United States and Great Britain* (Philadelphia, 1844); Charles J. Ingersoll, *Historical Sketch of the Second War Between the United States and Great Britain* (Philadelphia, 1845).

[3] Henry Adams, *The War of 1812*, ed. H. A. DeWeerd (Washington, 1944); John B. McMaster, *History of the People of the United States*, III (New York, 1892); Richard Hildreth, *The History of the United States of America from the Adoption of the Federal Constitution to the End of the Sixteenth Congress*, II and III (New York, 1874); Hermann E. von Holst, *The Constitutional and Political History of the United States*, I (Chicago, 1881); James Schouler, *History of the United States of America Under the Constitution*, II (New York, 1882).

[4] D. R. Anderson, "The Insurgents of 1811," American Historical Association, *Annual Report*, I (1911), 167; Howard T. Lewis, "A Re-Analysis of the Causes of the War of 1812," *Americana*, VI (1911), 506-16, 577-85.

[5] Louis M. Hacker, "Western Land Hunger and the War of 1812: A Conjecture," *Mississippi Valley Historical Review*, X (March, 1924), 365-95; Julius W. Pratt, "Western War Aims in the War of 1812," *Mississippi Valley Historical Review*, XII (June, 1925), 36-50; George R. Taylor, "Agrarian Discontent in the Mississippi Valley Preceding the War of 1812," *Journal of Political Economy*, XXXIX (August, 1931), 471-505; Reginald Horsman, "Who Were the War Hawks?" *Indiana Magazine of History*, LX (June, 1964), 121-36; Norman K. Risjord, "1812: Conservatives, War-Hawks and the Nation's Honor," *William and Mary Quarterly*, 3d series, XVIII (April, 1961), 196-211; Bernard Mayo, *Henry Clay, Spokesman of the New West* (Boston, 1937); Charles M. Wiltse, *John C. Calhoun: Nationalist, 1782-1828* (Indianapolis, 1944).

to bring about a declaration of war, an effort was made to posit an alliance between West and South based on complementary imperialistic ambitions and common economic depression.[6]

The inevitable result has been the acceptance of all of these factors as having played some role in developing war sentiment. This is, in effect, a multicausal solution which suggests that without the maritime controversy the war would not have occurred.[7] The most recent study of the causes of the War of 1812, Roger Brown's *The Republic in Peril,* accepts all of the causes which other historians have advanced[8] and asserts that these factors were important because their very existence threatened the United States' republican experiment. The seeming inability of the United States to protect its frontiers against Indian uprisings, and to protect its economy against the maritime depredations of the two European belligerents tended to prove the dire predictions of the post-Revolutionary War Cassandras who had warned that republican institutions could not long endure persistent pressure. The United States went to war to protect the reputation of republicanism.

To Brown, the important characteristic of the vote for war was not its sectional, but its partisan character. All the Federalists voted against war; a preponderant majority

[6] Julius W. Pratt, *The Expansionists of 1812* (New York, 1925); Margaret K. Latimer, "South Carolina, Protagonist of the War of 1812," *American Historical Review,* LXI (July, 1955), 914-30.

[7] Reginald Horsman, *The Causes of the War of 1812* (Philadelphia, 1962); Bradford Perkins, *Prologue to War: England and the United States, 1805-1812* (Berkeley, 1961); A. L. Burt, *Great Britain, the United States and British North America from the Revolution to the Establishment of Peace After the War of 1812* (New Haven, Conn., 1940).

[8] Brown denies the existence of a definable or identifiable group of war hawks, *The Republic in Peril* (New York, 1964), 44-47. See also Roger H. Brown, "The War Hawks of 1812: An Historical Myth," *Indiana Magazine of History,* LX (June, 1964), 137-50.

of Republicans voted for it.[9] Brown argues that the Republicans, determined to show the world that republicanism could succeed and that a republican government could protect the national interest, brought about a declaration of war. To prove his thesis, he examines the attitudes and positions of Republican congressmen, administration officials, and local Republican leaders.

While Pennsylvania Republicans were concerned with the reputation of republican institutions, concern for the welfare and unity of the Republican party was a more immediate and pressing consideration. As American policy continued to drift, Pennsylvania Republicans feared that the administration's failure to take effective action to protect American rights might cause the people to seek new leadership. They pressed for a declaration of war to insure the Republican party's success in the elections of 1812.

Republicans believed that the Federalist opposition had little faith in republican institutions and that if the republican experiment were to be successful the Republican party must be in power. Events in the four years preceding the declaration of war indicate a resurgence of Federalist strength. The Republicans attributed this to the Federalist assertions that the nation's ambiguous foreign policy, deteriorating economy, and weak frontiers could only be saved by a return of Federalists to power. To prevent further growth of Federalist strength, to retain power in their hands, and thereby to assure friendly direction of the republican experiment, the Republicans took the nation to war. Pennsylvania, "The Keystone of the Democratic Arch," provided the largest vote in favor of war and gave willing and constant support to its prosecution, and both nationally and domestically was

[9] Brown, *The Republic in Peril*, 45.

more steadfastly Republican than any other state in the Union. None of the studies of the causes of the war gives more than passing attention to Pennsylvania, but an understanding of the factors which motivated Pennsylvania's representatives to vote for war sheds light on Republican attitudes.

CHAPTER ONE

Expansion as a
Cause for War

In 1890, Henry Adams suggested in his *History of the United States,* that the traditional maritime interpretations of the War of 1812 did not adequately explain the causes of that conflict. By 1902 the maritime interpretation had been sufficiently challenged to enable Woodrow Wilson to assert that the grounds for war were singularly uncertain. This uncertainty led students to an intensive, and as yet incomplete search for new and different explanations.[1]

Aware of the fact that most support for the war came from the West and the South, historians attempted to ascertain the factors which prompted these areas to favor war with Britain. Early explanations of western motives stressed expansionist desire for Canada, fear of British intrigue among the Indians, and a highly developed sense of national honor among settlers on the frontier. Different historians, selecting for emphasis various of these factors, produced a variety of combinations and explanations for the war and a major historiographical controversy developed concerning them.[2]

The issues in this controversy were clearly drawn, however, between those who argued that desire for Canada was based on land hunger, and those who argued that desire for Canada resulted from the westerner's conviction that the British incited and supplied the renewed Indian uprisings on the frontier. The revival of Richard Hildreth's contention that the conquest of Canada was a method of carrying on the war, not a cause of it, further complicated the issue.[3]

The most detailed study of western causes, Julius W. Pratt's *The Expansionists of 1812* temporarily settled the question of expansionist desire for Canada as a cause of the war. This study won general acceptance for the contention that British intrigue among the Indians, not land hunger, was the primary motive in the West's desire for war. Pratt realized that the West did not have enough votes or influence to bring about a declaration of war. He also had to explain the South's equally strong support. He asserted, but never proved satisfactorily, that the South wanted Florida as much as the West wanted Canada, and for much the same reason: fear of Anglo-Spanish intrigue among the Indians. He then posited a western-southern alliance in which congressmen from the two sections agreed to bring on a war through which each section could satisfy its ambitions: "There is good evidence

[1] Henry Adams, *History of the United States of America During the Administrations of Jefferson and Madison* (New York, 1889-1891), IV, 340, 307-15, VI, 237-43; Woodrow Wilson, *A History of the American People* (New York, 1902), III, 214.

[2] Howard T. Lewis, "A Re-Analysis of the Causes of the War of 1812," *Americana*, VI (1911), 506-16, 577-85; D. R. Anderson, "The Insurgents of 1811," American Historical Association, *Annual Report*, I (1911), 165-76; Louis M. Hacker, "Western Land Hunger and the War of 1812: A Conjecture," *Mississippi Valley Historical Review*, X (March, 1924), 365-95; Julius W. Pratt, "Western War Aims in the War of 1812," *Mississippi Valley Historical Review*, XII (June, 1925), 36-50.

[3] Richard Hildreth, *History of the United States of America* (New York, 1880), VI, 313. Reginald Horsman, "Western War Aims, 1811-1812," *Indiana Magazine of History*, LIII (January, 1957), 16; A. L. Burt, *The United States, Great Britain, and British North America* (New York, 1961), 310.

that before the declaration of war, northern and southern Republicans came to a definite understanding that the acquisition of Canada on the North was to be balanced by the acquisition of the Floridas on the South."[4]

Most historians who concern themselves with the western causes of the war include western Pennsylvania as a part of the West, but say little about that state's role in the drive for war. The question of whether fear of the Indians, a drive for Canadian land, or acquiescence in a sectional bargain existed in Pennsylvania must be answered if that state's support for the war is to be understood.

Pratt's contention that there was no mention of desire to annex Canada in order to add to agricultural acreage is valid. Of the newspapers consulted, only two issues mention annexation. There were only two items, and these were three years apart. In January 1809, the Pittsburgh *Commonwealth* reprinted an article from the Boston *Centinel* which advocated the annexation of Canada in order to weaken England and "add to the power and revenue of the United States."[5] Three years later, at a Fourth of July celebration the *Commonwealth* reported a toast "to Canada, may it soon be counted as another star in our political hemisphere." This toast was made after Madison had sent his war message and war sentiment had been greatly aroused.[6] The *Commonwealth* and other Pittsburgh newspapers report twelve other celebrations of that Independence Day at none of which were such annexationist sentiments expressed. The same is true of other reports of Fourth of July celebrations in the Washington *Reporter*, the Carlisle *Gazette*, the Philadelphia *Aurora*, the Pennsylvania *Gazette*, and the Pennsylvania *Republican* and Dauphin *Guardian*, both of Harrisburg.

There is, however, a great deal of evidence to the con-

[4] Julius W. Pratt, *The Expansionists of 1812* (New York, 1925), 13.
[5] Pittsburgh *Commonwealth*, Jan. 25, 1809.
[6] Pittsburgh *Commonwealth*, July 17, 1812.

trary. Some members of the Pennsylvania congressional delegation opposed annexation on the floor of the House, and none ever spoke in favor of it. John Smilie, the dean of the delegation in terms of age and years of service, announced that "we should be justified in carrying [a war] into the enemy's territory only in order to bring it to a speedy conclusion." William Findley, a representative from western Pennsylvania, opposed taking any territory "unless it became necessary in our own defence." William Milnor, Adam Seybert of Philadelphia, and Joseph Lefever all spoke against annexation.[7]

If they mentioned it at all, the newspapers also opposed annexation. In a widely reprinted article opposing naval expansion, the *Aurora* argued that a navy is an offensive weapon "calculated to extend territory," and asked, "Do we want to extend our soil when we already have more than we can cultivate?"[8] The Federalist Pennsylvania *Gazette* opposed annexation on the grounds that republican governments have no business undertaking a war of "plunder and rapine," and warned that any attempt to capture Canada would fail.[9] Even after the declaration of war it is difficult to find annexationist sentiment.

In June 1812, the House passed a resolution authorizing the president to issue a proclamation assuring the citizens of Canada protection of their "lives, property, and religion" if it should become necessary for the United States to invade their territory. The normally united Pennsylvania delegation opposed the measure 10 to 6, with two members not voting. In the Senate, where the House resolution was defeated, both Pennsylvania senators voted against it.[10]

[7] *Annals of Congress*, 10th Cong., 2d sess., 1360; 11th Cong., 2d sess., 1514, 1519; 12th Cong., 1st sess., 609, 813.

[8] Philadelphia *Aurora*, Oct. 11, 1811.

[9] Pennsylvania *Gazette* (Philadelphia), Oct. 1, 1811; Pennsylvania *Republican* (Harrisburg), April 7, 1812.

[10] *Annals of Congress*, 12th Cong., 1st sess., 323, 607.

Pratt's statement that land hunger could not have been a cause for war because there was abundant unsettled land awaiting cultivation also proves true for Pennsylvania. There was a great deal of unsettled land available in the westernmost counties of the state. Erie, Butler, Venango, Warren, and Crawford counties each had a population of less than nine thousand and the average was less than forty-five hundred.[11] Much of this land was in the hands of speculators, but it was available to farmers. The reports of the state auditor and treasurer show that the state sold large amounts of land in the six years preceding the war. These were sales of relatively small lots, usually between $0.80 and $1.00 per acre, and never in excess of $1.25 per acre.[12]

Expansion was thus unnecessary for Pennsylvania farmers because small farms were profitable and land was available. A Pittsburgh traveler marveled at the "great farms of 230 acres which produced 11,000 bushels of wheat" he had seen on a trip through Ohio and Indiana.[13] The average in Warren County was between 100 and 150 acres, and most farms had less than 100 acres. Warren County was sparsely settled and farms were smaller in the southern and eastern counties. John Kraus made a yearly profit on a 75-acre farm in central Pennsylvania.[14]

Pratt's thesis that land hunger was not responsible for war sentiment in Pennsylvania is corroborated by a review of the situations existing in that state, but similar study does not support his contention that preoccupation with the Indian danger and suspicion of hostile British support of the Indians explain the West's desire for war with

[11] *Pennsylvania Senate Journal,* 1810-1811, appendix I (Harrisburg, 1834-1837).

[12] Income from the sale of state lands can be found in table II, page 38, below.

[13] *Cramer's Pittsburgh Almanac* (Pittsburgh, 1811), 51-52.

[14] John S. Schenck, ed., *History of Warren County, Pennsylvania* (Syracuse, 1887), 127-30; John Kraus, account books, 1806-1809.

England.[15] Some Pennsylvanians expressed fear of the Indians, but they did not always connect Indian uprisings with British intrigue. Others denied that they felt threatened at all. The Wyoming Massacre of 1788 marked the end of serious Indian problems in the state, and the last recorded Indian murder in Pennsylvania west of Pittsburgh occurred in 1790. Other histories of the state, as well as histories of other counties, indicate that there was little concern with the Indian menace until the summer of 1807.[16]

News of the *Chesapeake* incident produced reports of Indian murders, all of which suggested an alliance between the British and the savages. The Pittsburgh *Commonwealth*, which had earlier supported a toast "to our Indian brethren" began to carry reports of Indian depredations, noting murders in Fort Wayne, Detroit, and Florida.

Between the end of July 1807 and the end of January 1808, the *Commonwealth* carried more reports of Indian incidents than it had in the two previous years. The reports, however, do not blame the British for the incidents. The only indication that Benjamin Brown, the editor, even considered this possibility was an article reprinted from the Philadelphia *Aurora* calling for the annexation of Canada in order to end Indian hostility.[17]

Other newspapers, which also increased their coverage of Indian affairs after the *Chesapeake* incident, emphasized the connection between the Indians and the British.[18] The Carlisle *Gazette* stated that a traveler from

15 Pratt, "Western War Aims," 50.
16 Henderson Bausman, *History of Beaver County* (New York, 1904), 166-69; Howard M. Jenkins, *Pennsylvania, Colonial and Federal* (Philadelphia, 1903), II, 187; Catherine E. Reiser, *Pittsburgh's Commercial Development* (Harrisburg, 1951), 4.
17 Pittsburgh *Commonwealth*, Sept. 16, 1807.
18 Pittsburgh *Gazette*, Aug. 4, Oct. 13, Dec. 5, 1807; Washington *Reporter*, Aug. 16, Sept. 9, 1807, Jan. 4, 1808; Carlisle *Gazette*, Aug. 9, Aug. 16, 1807; Dauphin *Guardian*, Sept. 8, Oct. 6, 1807.

Detroit reported that the prevailing opinion of the British was that there would be war. He accused the British of generously supplying and keeping ready about three thousand warriors who would undertake a general massacre when war was declared.[19] The *Guardian* warned that the first effect of war with Britain would be a savage frontier war against Indians supported by the British. The *Aurora* published reports that the British were pouring men and arms into Canada. With every increase in the British force, there was a proportionate increase in Indian activity on both the northern and southern frontiers. The editor, William Duane, told his readers that the nation would never be free of Indian wars until the British were driven from the continent.[20]

However, the evidence refuting Pratt's thesis is strong. The number of incidents on the frontier did not increase in the summer and fall of 1807, nor did British aid to the Indians increase in the period.[21] The heightened interest in Indian affairs and the efforts to connect the British with the Indian uprisings are more indicative of a rush of anti-British feeling resulting from the *Chesapeake* affair than of a growing fear of the Indians.

Although the press became more concerned with the Indians, other evidence indicates a continuing lack of fear of the Indians. The debates in the state legislature exhibit no fear for safety of the state's frontiers. The senate did receive one petition from a militia division in the western part of the state requesting increased protection from the Indians. Neither the petition nor the senate debate mention any British influence among the Indians. The senate did pass a bill for the "defence of the northern and western

[19] Carlisle *Gazette,* Jan. 8, 1808; Dauphin *Guardian,* Sept. 15, Oct. 20, 1807; Harrisburg *Times,* Sept. 28, 1807.

[20] July 1, July 9, 1807.

[21] Reginald Horsman, *The Causes of the War of 1812* (Philadelphia, 1962), 159, 169-71.

frontier" by a very narrow margin, but the house did not even consider it.[22] In the same session the Pennsylvania house denied a petition from the citizens of Erie County asking to be given arms to defend themselves against the Indians on the grounds that the danger was "remote." Again, neither the petition nor the house debate refer to an Anglo-Indian alliance.[23] In every session after 1805 the Pennsylvania legislature passed resolutions approving the conduct of foreign affairs by the national government. Every one of these resolutions listed grievances against England, but only the resolution passed in December 1812 mentioned the Indians as a grievance.[24]

In Washington, William Findley was the only representative from Pennsylvania who mentioned Indian troubles during the Tenth Congress. Arguing against postponing consideration of a bill to increase the military establishment, he stated that on the northwestern frontier "the alarm is considerable and the danger apparent." As proof he cited the previously mentioned bill passed by the state senate. In this speech he did not try to implicate the British.[25]

By the end of February 1808, when excitement over the *Chesapeake* incident abated, concern with the Indian problem subsided also. From the spring of 1808 until the summer of 1811 there were few references to Indian hostilities in the Pennsylvania press. Most of these were simply reprints from western and southern newspapers.

As news of the Wabash confederation drifted eastward, interest in Indian affairs surpassed the 1807 level by the summer of 1811. Republican newspapers made no effort · to explain the renewed Indian hostility, concentrating

[22] *Pennsylvania Senate Journal,* 1807-1808, pp. 231-32, 274.
[23] *Pennsylvania House Journal,* 1807-1808, pp. 181-82.
[24] *Pennsylvania Senate Journal,* 1812-1813, p. 46.
[25] *Annals of Congress,* 10th Cong., 1st sess., 1521-22.

instead on a review of the "friendly," "just," and "honorable" Indian policy of Jefferson and Madison.[26]

Federalist newspapers, which devoted more space to Indian uprisings, made a distinct effort to blame the administration. The Federalist press contended that the Indians had not been treated fairly, and that there was justification for their hostility. These papers provided vivid pictures of the devastation and brutality of Indian warfare, suggesting that the situation would worsen if the United States declared war against them or against Great Britain.[27] Neither Republicans nor Federalists tried to associate the British with the resurgent Indian uprisings during the summer and early fall of 1811. This attitude, of course, changed drastically with news of the battle of Tippecanoe.

The Republican press blamed the entire affair on the British and echoed the sentiment of the *Aurora* that there could be no security against the savages until the British were driven from Canada.[28] The Federalist press attempted to explain away the evidence of British aid by arguing that British weapons had been planted among the Indians by Americans in order to create further excitement and agitation against Great Britain. Another explanation was that Indian hostilities had been incited by greedy land speculators who knew that the Indians would be defeated and driven from their land.[29]

William Findley explained that he would vote in favor of the increase in the military establishment proposed by the foreign relations committee because the situation on

[26] Pittsburgh *Commonwealth*, Aug. 7, 1811; Carlisle *Gazette*, July 29, 1811; Washington *Reporter*, July 23, 1811; Pittsburgh *Mercury*, July 23, 1811; Philadelphia *Aurora*, June 18, June 23, July 22, 1811.
[27] Pittsburgh *Gazette*, Sept. 29, Oct. 23, Nov. 6, 1811; Pennsylvania *Gazette* (Philadelphia), Sept. 9, Sept. 23, Oct. 17, Nov. 16, 1811.
[28] Philadelphia *Aurora*, Dec. 14, 1811.
[29] Pittsburgh *Gazette*, Dec. 19, 1811, Jan. 16, Jan. 23, July 24, 1812; Pennsylvania *Gazette*, Jan. 15, Jan. 22, Feb. 5, July 9, 1812.

the frontier demanded it. Admitting that "we have at present no such explicit proof [as in 1794] that the Indians . . . are acting as British allies, yet we have as much proof as the nature of the case can afford." It should be noted, however, that of the six other Pennsylvania representatives who spoke in favor of the report, not one supported it on similar grounds. Findley said that threats of taking Canada were improper.[30]

By the end of 1811 concern with the Indian problem again subsided and there were few reports of Indian hostility until April 1812. In that month the press began to devote considerable space to Indian massacres, the coverage growing more complete in May and early June. Still, there was no attempt to link the renewal of the Indian wars with the British in Canada.[31] Evidently, the renewed Indian activity was considered a part of the intermittent frontier war rather than the result of British aggression and intrigue.[32]

It could be expected that the British would have been blamed for the Indian war during this period even if no evidence existed to prove it. The fact that they were not indicates that the people were more concerned with the Indian than with any alleged Anglo-Indian alliance. Even the governor of Pennsylvania reflected this attitude. In his general orders for the drafting and organization of the fourteen thousand militia which the president had ordered into federal service, the governor devoted a great deal of attention to maritime grievances, but only one sentence to the Indian menace.[33]

The Washington *Reporter,* one of the few important newspapers between Pittsburgh and the Ohio border, pro-

[30] *Annals of Congress,* 12th Cong., 1st sess., 499-502.
[31] Pittsburgh *Commonwealth,* April 28, May 19, June 9, June 23, 1812; Pittsburgh *Gazette,* March 20, April 17, June 12, 1812.
[32] Pittsburgh *Commonwealth,* May 2, May 5, 1812.
[33] *Pennsylvania Archives,* 2d series, XII, 557.

vides a good index to shifting attitudes toward the Indians. More than any other Pennsylvania newspaper, it reprinted articles reporting Indian incidents from Ohio and Indiana newspapers, but it took little cognizance of these events in its own columns. The *Reporter* was a prowar newspaper and never missed a chance to list United States grievances against England or demand that the United States protect its rights, honor, and independence. Every catalog of American grievances includes impressment, blockades, the orders-in-council, and specific maritime incidents. With the exception of a few issues after the *Chesapeake* affair, and again after the battle of Tippecanoe, neither the Anglo-Indian alliance nor Indian hostility is included in the *Reporter*'s lists from 1806 to June 1812.

The Cumberland *Register* followed a similar pattern. Archibald Laudon, its editor, published a work entitled "A Selection of Some of the Most Interesting Narratives of Outrages Committed by the Indians in Their Wars with the White People." He advertised it constantly in his paper, published portions of it in some of which he accused the British of inciting the Indians during the 1790s and carried regular dispatches about current Indian attacks. Not once in the years 1808 to 1812, did he connect Indian uprisings on the frontier with British intrigue or hostility. It seems, then, that before the war concern with British intrigue among the Indians was not an overriding concern with Pennsylvania.

As soon as the war began, however, stories of past and present Indian atrocities became numerous and evidence was produced to prove that Indian hostilities had been instigated by the British. The Pittsburgh *Commonwealth,* commenting on the savagery with which the Indians waged war, insisted that "every man . . . well remembers that for many months preceding the declaration of war our western border had witnessed similar scenes [of destruction] and the fact was established that *even in peace*

a price was paid for these murders by the British. . . .
Every schoolboy knows that the encouragement of these
butcheries was one of the *causes* instead of being an *effect*
of war." It warned that only a victory under the leadership of President Madison could bring peace to the frontier. Those who demanded the election of Clinton in the
naïve belief that the signing of a peace would end the
atrocities had forgotten the past. Peace on the frontier
could only be assured by driving the British from Canada.[34]

Richard Rush, comptroller general of the United States
in the early part of the war, spoke strongly to his friend
Charles J. Ingersoll: "I would not make peace while a
single vestige of impressment or the Indian question
remained unsatisfied. . . . What a magnificent provocation
and justification of war they present! What are the Nookta
sounds, the Falkland Islands . . . the taxation without
representation—aye even this—what the three pence a
pound on tea, all the questions and entanglements about
limits, ceremonies, navigations, trade, burning ships at
sea, monopolies and all the other puny causes . . . compared with the naked enormity of these two."[35] British
use of Indian savages, Rush insisted, presented new problems in America's relationship with England. He felt that
this was a question which required perfect understanding
before negotiations were begun: "I mean the employment
of the Indian force. . . . My language then would be to
Britain disavow explicitly this act of your deputies in
Canada and give us the most absolute guarantee that it
will never be done in the future." Until such a guarantee
were received the United States would be forced to con-

---

[34] Pittsburgh *Commonwealth,* Oct. 6, 1812. See also the Philadelphia
Aurora, Nov. 11, 1812; Carlisle *Gazette,* Dec. 2, 1812; Washington *Reporter,* Oct. 11, 1812, for similar statements.

[35] Richard Rush to Charles J. Ingersoll, Dec. 20, 1812, Charles J.
Ingersoll Papers, Historical Society of Pennsylvania, Philadelphia. Hereafter cited as Ingersoll Papers.

tinue the war.[36] Correspondents of Jonathan Roberts, another representative from Pennsylvania, and the Pennsylvania press expressed similar sentiments after the declaration of war.

Another reason for taking Canada was produced after hostilities began. Referring to the Henry[37] attempts to foment civil war in New England, the Carlisle *Gazette* demanded "the severing of Canada from the British empire." The editorial maintained that if Canada were to be used as a base for sowing dissention among the states it could not be allowed to remain under British rule. In a letter complaining of congressional immobility Edward Fox told Jonathan Roberts that the Henry affair was "a most fortunate discovery," because "the actual fixing of interference of the British government must put ours on a strong ground." Joseph Burke wrote Roberts concerning the Henry affair: "Until within a very few days I would not permit myself to believe that there was any danger of a war with England . . . at this time but I confess that my opinion is now verging to the contrary side." Roberts, himself, felt the papers Henry mentioned were "ample proof of the consummate perfidity and iniquity" of the British government.[38] The resolutions of the Pennsylvania legislature cite the attempt "to kindle dissatisfaction, dis-

[36] Rush to Ingersoll, Nov. 15, 1812, Ingersoll Papers.

[37] Henry was alleged to be a British agent sent to New England to persuade Federalists to detach the area from the United States. Failing to do that he sold his papers to the Republican administration under circumstances that are still mysterious. Madison then used the inconclusive information bought from Henry to attack the Federalists and referred to it in his war message. Henry Adams contended that this incident was not significant in the development of war sentiment, but the evidence indicates that at least in Pennsylvania, the Henry disclosures aroused some indignation. See Adams, *History*, IV, 179-84.

[38] Carlisle *Gazette*, March 20, 1812; Philadelphia *Aurora*, July 2, 1812; Dauphin *Guardian*, Dec. 18, 1810; Edward Fox to Jonathan Roberts, March 18, 1812; Joseph Burke to Jonathan Roberts, March 20, 1812; Jonathan Roberts to Matthew Roberts, March 14, 1812. The Roberts correspondence is found in the Jonathan Roberts Papers, Historical Society of Pennsylvania, Philadelphia. Hereafter cited as Roberts Papers.

cord, rebellion, and civil war" by use of "secret emmisaries
sent from Canada" as a cause for war. The governor
also alluded to the "discord sown amongst our people
by an accredited agent of the British government" in his
general orders to detached militia.[39] Neither the legislature nor the governor mentioned this incident in their
prewar pronouncements.

British intrigue among the Indians or desire to drive the
British out of Canada for other reasons did not become a
cause of the war until after it was declared. The Anglo-
Indian connection and British possession of Canada were
used by the Republicans as political issues to discredit the
Clintonians in the presidential campaign of 1812, and as
an excuse for continuing the war after one of the avowed
cause for declaring it, the orders-in-council, had been
removed.

Pratt also suggests that British competition in the fur
trade played a role in developing prowar sentiment, the
hope being that with the British expelled from Canada,
United States interests would gain complete control of the
fur trade.[40] Around the turn of the century Pittsburgh had ·
been a major center of the fur trade. Colonel James
O'Hara was successful in the business, getting most of his
pelts from the Indians.[41] At that time complete control
of the fur trade would have been welcome to the citizens
of Pittsburgh. One of his western factors told O'Hara
that he hoped "England might be driven from this
trade."[42] As fur traders moved to more fruitful areas west
of the Mississippi, Pittsburgh lost its position as a major

[39] *Pennsylvania Senate Journal*, 1812-1813, p. 46; *Pennsylvania Archives*, 2d series, XII, 557. The most detailed account of the Henry affair
is in "The Henry-Crillon Affair of 1812" in Samuel Eliot Morison's *By
Land and by Sea* (New York, 1954), 265-86.
[40] Pratt, *Expansionists of 1812*, pp. 27, 188.
[41] Joseph McFerron to Col. James O'Hara, June 20, 1802, Denny-
O'Hara Papers, Western Pennsylvania Historical Society, Pittsburgh.
Hereafter cited as Denny-O'Hara Papers.
[42] McFerron to O'Hara, Nov. 8, 1800, Denny-O'Hara Papers.

center of the trade, and by 1810 furs ceased to play an important role in the city's economy. Neither *Cramer's Pittsburgh Almanac,* nor the Pittsburgh *Directory* listed fur trade as an important business, and there was no mention of it in the press or the speeches of Pennsylvania congressmen.[43] Evidently, the fur trade was no longer important to the state's economy, nor was it a factor in determining attitudes towards war.

Historians studying other sections of the country, or the development of American attitudes have also been dissatisfied with Pratt's explanation. They account for the prominent position Canada held in the correspondence, speeches, and newspapers of the day by reviving Hildreth's suggestion that an attack on Canada was to be a method of fighting the war, not an object of it.[44] Many Pennsylvanians who had no desire for more land and no fear of the Indians favored an attack on Canada as a tactical objective. In the available correspondence of the period, this theme is more prevalent than any other.

Soon after the *Chesapeake* incident, Jesse Higgins wrote Jonathan Roberts that if Britain did not disavow the action and assure American rights, the United States would have to fight. "The principal means of annoyance in our power is the seizure of Canada and sequestration of British debts."[45] Findley's speech opposing an attack on Canada concludes that offensive operations are the best way to carry on defensive war. The nation had been attacked from Canada before, he warned the House, and might well be again. If the appropriation for increasing the militia and the regular force were not passed the presi-

[43] *Cramer's Pittsburgh Almanac,* 1811, also 1812, 1813, 1814.

[44] Hildreth, *History,* VI, 313-14; Horsman, *Causes of the War of 1812,* 184; Roger H. Brown, *The Republic in Peril* (New York, 1964), 119; Burt, *The United States, Great Britain, and British North America,* 309-10; Bradford Perkins, *Prologue to War* (Berkeley, 1961), 426.

[45] Jesse Higgins to Jonathan Roberts, July 19, 1807, Roberts Papers.

dent would be unable to use national force to prevent invasion.[46] Later in the session Findley returned to the same argument. After being asked to explain a vote he had cast in 1794 in favor of naval armaments in view of his present opposition to naval expansion, Findley told the House that in 1794 he had favored expansion of the navy and opposed expansion of the army because the most likely enemy, France, could only be attacked at sea. Now (1810) the situation was reversed. The United States, he claimed, was unfit to match the enemy at sea, but could inflict great harm on Britain simply by marching its army over the Canadian border.[47] Similarly Senator Andrew Gregg wrote William Jones that he opposed war, but that if it must come, he considered Britain the enemy because it was the first and greatest aggressor and because the United States had power to retaliate by attacking Canada and harassing Britain's commerce.[48]

In the winter and spring of 1812 demands for an attack on Canada increased and, after war was declared, they became even more insistent. Arguing in favor of the report of the foreign relations committee, Jonathan Roberts supported an increase in the regular force because he felt an attack on Canada would be effective, and his opinion was supported by constituents and friends in Pennsylvania. John Connelly, a Republican member of the Pennsylvania legislature, wrote that he approved of Roberts' opposition to naval expansion because no matter how large a navy the United States constructed it would never match England's. A large army, on the other hand, would be essential if the nation were to attack Great Britain in Canada, where it was most vulnerable. James

[46] *Annals of Congress,* 11th Cong., 2d sess., 1519.
[47] *Annals of Congress,* 11th Cong., 2d sess., 1528.
[48] Andrew Gregg to William Jones, April 10, 1810, William Jones Papers, Historical Society of Pennsylvania, Philadelphia. Hereafter cited as Jones Papers.

Evans, a member of the Pennsylvania House of Representatives, informed Roberts that many legislators saw no
way to fight the war except by an attack on Canada.[49]

Discussing demands for a war against France as well as
England, William Jones told Roberts that "even if the
aggravations of the two powers were so equal that a
feather would turn the scale, practical considerations
would point to that foe whose commerce contiguity of
territory and internal resources we can most effectively
assail." Great Britain qualified on these points.[50]

The Philadelphia *Aurora* summed up the opinion of the
press when it told its readers that they should not "in-
quire or calculate how many millions the conquest of
Canada will put into the treasury of the U.S." Rather,
they should ask "what injury this conquest will do our
enemy . . . and what we may gain by a restoration . . .
at the conclusion of a peace."[51] Richard Rush wrote
Ingersoll that the capture of Canada was "the path of
safety, honor, popularity, triumphs." The victory of our
arms in Canada would greatly retrieve "the honor lost in
years of docile submission."[52] The Pittsburgh *Mercury*
announced that "the road to a lasting and honorable peace
lies through Canada."[53]

Defending his party against Federalist attacks that the
Canadian campaign had turned the war from a defensive
to an offensive one, Charles J. Ingersoll argued that a good
offense had always been the best defense, and that the
fact that we had undertaken offensive operations did not

[49] *Annals of Congress*, 12th Cong., 1st sess., 502-506; Connelly to
Roberts, Feb. 26, 1812, J. Evans to Roberts and Abner Lacock, March ?,
1812, Roberts Papers; Newman Dorland, "The Second Troop of Philadelphia City Cavalry," *Pennsylvania Magazine of History and Biography*,
XLIX (January, 1925), 182n.
[50] William Jones to Jonathan Roberts, May 27, 1812, Jones Papers.
[51] Philadelphia *Aurora*, July 8, 1812.
[52] Richard Rush to C. J. Ingersoll, Dec. 20, 1812, Ingersoll Papers.
[53] Pittsburgh *Mercury*, Jan. 21, 1813.

necessarily mean that we were engaged in offensive war. The object had not been territorial aggrandizement, but tactical and strategic advantage. The attack on Canada was the best way to "make our mighty foe sensible of American power."[54]

While the evidence is not conclusive, it strongly suggests that the portion of Pratt's thesis which deals with Canada and the Indians does not apply to Pennsylvania. Yet, many Pennsylvanians who would not go to war to acquire Canada did believe that if a war had to be fought, an attack on Canada promised the best possibility of bringing it to a swift and victorious conclusion.[55]

Pratt's second major proposition, that southern desire for Florida made possible a prowar alliance between southern and western congressmen, has been generally repudiated. A close study of Pennsylvania sources substantiates this repudiation. There is simply no evidence that desire for Florida, or acquiescence in a sectional bargain in any way prompted Pennsylvania's support for the war. During the war there was some sentiment for taking Florida to deny Britain a strategically important possession, but this was a tactical consideration, not a cause of the war.[56] There was no mention of Florida in connection with war against Britain before the war.

There was, however, a very real desire for Florida in Pennsylvania, but the desire was not a motivation for war. Pennsylvania congressmen strongly supported Madison's occupation of West Florida in October 1810, and in a

[54] C. J. Ingersoll, *Historical Sketch of the Second War Between the United States and Great Britain,* 2 vols. (Philadelphia, 1845-1849), II, 17-18.

[55] See Connelly to Roberts, April 25, May 21, May 26, 1812, Fox to Roberts, April 19, 1812, Roberts Papers.

[56] Burt, *The United States, Great Britain, and British North America,* 306; Horsman, "Western War Aims," 15; Margaret K. Latimer, "South Carolina, Protagonist of the War of 1812," *American Historical Review,* LXI (July, 1955), 927.

later session of the Eleventh Congress voted in favor of
legislation authorizing him to take East Florida.[57] Fifteen
of the state's eighteen congressmen invariably voted with
the administration. In all, twenty-seven ballots were taken
on the Florida question in a secret session, and on each
one the delegation split 15-3, with Milnor, Jenkins, and
Heister (the last two were the only Federalists in the
delegation) always voting with the minority.[58] When
this debate was made public the Republican press in
Pennsylvania unanimously approved the decision of Congress and the votes of the state's Republican representatives. This strong support for occupation and eventual
annexation of the Spanish possession only reflects loyalty
to a cherished Republican dream for possession of the
Floridas and cannot be produced as evidence as a cause
for the war. It was but another effort to take Florida
which occurred concurrently with other factors which
were bringing on war.[59]

Briefly, then, it can be stated that Pratt's thesis does not
apply to Pennsylvania because neither desire for Canada
or Florida nor fear of the Indians prompted Pennsylvania's
support for the war.

[57] *Annals of Congress,* 11th Cong., 3d sess., 369-70, 1117.
[58] The House debate can be found in the *Annals of Congress,* 11th
Cong., 3d sess., 1117-47.
[59] Burt, *The United States, Great Britain, and British North America,*
306-10; Isaac Cox, *The West Florida Controversy, 1798-1813* (Baltimore,
1918).

CHAPTER TWO

Economic Depression as
a Cause for War

Julius Pratt's analysis of the factors which prompted the West and the South to support the War of 1812 left so many questions unanswered and created so many new problems that new approaches had to be found. The revisionist interpretation concentrated more on economic than political factors.

George R. Taylor broke new ground in two articles describing economic conditions on the frontier. He concluded that "western agriculture suffered . . . a severe economic depression in the years just before the war, and this depression was an important factor in determining the support which the frontier gave first to the embargo and nonintercourse, and finally to war."[1] Although he draws very little of his evidence from Pennsylvania sources, he includes the western part of the state in his frontier.[2]

Taking her cue from Taylor, Margaret K. Latimer studied economic conditions in South Carolina and concluded that war sentiment in that state resulted from a disastrous depression in the price of cotton which the planters blamed on Britain's commercial restrictions. She strongly implied that her findings could be applied to the

whole cotton South and further intimated that it was not
a political alliance, but the common bond of economic
disaster that united western and southern congressmen
behind the administration's foreign policy and drove
Madison to demand war.[3]

This economic interpretation has received better treat-
ment from historians than Pratt's theories. Two of the
most reputable histories of Pennsylvania uncritically accept this economic analysis and apply it to the entire
state.[4] However, close study of economic conditions in
Pennsylvania reveals that the state, including the western
counties, did not suffer a depression between 1808 and
1812. On the contrary, most indications are that the
period was one of increasing prosperity, thus Pennsylvania's support of the war cannot be attributed to economic depression.

In his *Early Western Pennsylvania Politics* Russell
Ferguson cites antiembargo articles and editorials from
the Pittsburgh *Gazette* to prove that the prices dropped
and economic conditions reached depression levels. The
Gazette, however, was a Federalist newspaper and its
editor, John Scull, might well have had partisan reasons
for opposing the embargo.

In the spring of 1807 hemp sold for six dollars per
hundredweight. After the passage of the embargo the
price rose to seven dollars per hundredweight. A variety

[1] George R. Taylor, "Prices in the Mississippi Valley Preceding the War of 1812," *Journal of Economic and Business History*, III (1930-1931), 471.

[2] George R. Taylor, "Agrarian Discontent in the Mississippi Valley Preceding the War of 1812," *Journal of Political Economy*, XXXIX (August, 1931), 475, 481.

[3] Margaret K. Latimer, "South Carolina, Protagonist of the War of 1812," *American Historical Review*, LXI (July, 1955), 914-30.

[4] Russell J. Ferguson, *Early Western Pennsylvania Politics* (Pittsburgh, 1938), 202-203; Sanford W. Higginbotham, *The Keystone of the Democratic Arch: Pennsylvania Politics 1800-1816* (Harrisburg, 1952), 258.

of factors, from normal seasonal swings to changes in demand, can account for this change, but the price rise indicates that hemp cultivators in western Pennsylvania were not adversely affected by the embargo. Cursory glances at the price of hemp from the passage of the embargo to the declaration of war show that it remained high throughout the period and rose sharply during the war.[5] Other farm staples show a similar price stability.

Barley sold at fifty-three cents per bushel throughout 1806, 1807, 1808, fell to forty-seven cents per bushel in September 1808, and remained at that price until April 1809.[6] After that date there are no quotations of prices, but the Pittsburgh Point brewery advertised in local papers that it would pay high prices for barley.[7] While the price of barley did drop after passage of the embargo, it was still a marketable product. Furthermore, there is no indication that the embargo can be blamed for the declining price. Barley was not a major export crop and could only be indirectly affected by the vicissitudes of American trade. Timothy Pitkin does not mention barley as an export item in his statistical compendium.[8] The 10 percent decline in the price of Pennsylvania barley is slight compared with the price declines in the Mississippi Valley, and did not cause a depression for barley growers.

Rye sold for nearly forty-five cents per bushel both before and after the embargo, and remained at that price until June 1812 when it reached fifty cents. It remained

[5] Pittsburgh *Gazette,* April 14-28, 1807, Dec. 7, 1808–April 12, 1809. For other quotations of the price of hemp, see Pittsburgh *Commonwealth,* June 18, 1807, Jan. 23, 1808, July 13, 1810, Jan. 21, Jan. 28, 1813; Washington *Reporter,* July 9, 1807, Jan. 5, 1810, Feb. 17, 1813.

[6] Pittsburgh *Gazette,* Aug. 26–Nov. 4, 1806, Aug. 18–Nov. 17, 1808, Jan. 12–April 12, 1808. Compare with Sept. 14, 1808–March 22, 1809.

[7] Ibid., Dec. 20, 1810, Nov. 23, 1811; Pittsburgh *Commonwealth,* Jan. 21, 1812, for example.

[8] Timothy Pitkin, *A Statistical View of the Commerce of the United States of America* (New Haven, 1835).

at fifty cents for most of the war period. There were, of course, fluctuations, but these were seasonal changes and show no relationship to political events. In fact the rise to fifty cents per bushel so soon after the passage of the ninety-day embargo in April 1812 seems to indicate that the status of America's commerce did not have a detrimental effect on the price of rye.[9] This figure must be used with caution, however, because rye prices are not cited regularly before 1812, and there are not enough figures to establish a definitive price schedule.

Prices for shelled corn and wheat followed a similar pattern. Corn, which sold for forty-two cents in the summer and fall of 1807, remained at that price after the embargo until the spring of 1812 when it rose to forty-five cents. By summer it sold for fifty cents per bushel.[10] Again, there is no relationship between the price of corn and the passage of commercial legislation except that significant price rises followed passage of the ninety-day embargo and the declaration of war.

Wheat fluctuated from seventy to seventy-five cents per bushel through the summer of 1807 to May 1811 when it dropped to a low of sixty-seven cents. The price remained depressed until June of 1812 when it rose to seventy-five cents and after the war, it rose to one dollar per bushel.[11]

The prices of staples in western Pennsylvania remained high because there was an adequate domestic market

[9] Pittsburgh *Gazette*, Sept. 9, 1807, Jan. 3, 1808, March 16, 1810, Jan. 24–June 5, 1812; Pittsburgh *Commonwealth*, June 16, 1807, Jan. 24, 1808, May 16, 1810, June 15–Oct. 6, 1812.

[10] Pittsburgh *Gazette*, Aug. 14, Nov. 11, 1807, Feb. 3, 1808, March 16, 1809, Jan. 24–March 13, March 20–June 5, Sept. 11–Nov. 4, 1812; Pittsburgh *Commonwealth*, June 12–Aug. 18, Sept. 1–Nov. 4, 1812.

[11] Pittsburgh *Gazette*, Aug. 14, 1807, Nov. 11, 1807, Jan. 23, 1808, Oct. 19, 1810, Feb. 1, Feb. 8, Feb. 15, 1811, Jan. 24–June 5, June 12–July 31, Aug. 8–Oct. 2, 1812; Pittsburgh *Commonwealth*, Sept. 7, Nov. 4, 1807, Feb. 11, 1808, July 15, 1811–June 9, Sept. 1–Oct. 6, 1812.

for them.[12]   What could not be sold in Pittsburgh could be easily disposed of in Ohio, Kentucky, and Tennessee.[13] The Pittsburgh area also served as an entrepot for much trade with the upper Mississippi Valley.[14]   Obviously, the farmers of western Pennsylvania were not adversely • affected by the commercial legislation of Jefferson and Madison.

The same is true of the rest of the state.   An index of • wholesale commodity prices in Philadelphia which was based on a study of twenty commodities provides interesting figures.   The index fluctuated from a high of 125 in January 1807 to a low of 115 in May, June, and July of that year, reaching 120 in the two months preceding the embargo.   Wholesale commodity prices declined precipitously in the first half of 1808 reaching a low of 103 in August.   They began to rise the same month and continued rising to a high of 142 in February 1811.   The index remains relatively high until after the declaration of war, when it begins to soar, reaching 186 in December of 1813 and 200 a year later.[15]   Other statistical studies substantiate these figures.[16]   Stock market prices quoted in Paulson's *American Daily Advertiser* show surprising stability (see table I).   There were, of course, minor fluctuations, but these are in no way related to political or international events connected with the administra-

---

[12] *Cramer's Pittsburgh Almanac*, 1809, pp. 34-38, 1810, pp. 52-58; Erasmus Wilson, *Standard History of Pittsburgh* (Chicago, 1898), 148; J. M. Riddle, *Pittsburgh Directory* (Pittsburgh, 1815), 140.

[13] Wilson, *Pittsburgh*, 152-59.

[14] See Denny-O'Hara account book, Jan. 1809, May 1810, Feb. 1811; O'Hara to Reed, July 16, 1810; O'Hara to McFerron, Jan. 26, 1811, Denny-O'Hara Papers; Neville Craig to Isaac Craig, April 14, 1809, May 6, 1811, April 29, 1812, Isaac Craig Papers, Carnegie Library, Pittsburgh.

[15] Arthur H. Cole, *Wholesale Commodity Prices in the United States 1700-1861* (Cambridge, 1938), 140-41.

[16] Anne Bezanson, Robert Gray, and Miriam Hussey, *Wholesale Prices in Philadelphia 1784-1861* (Philadelphia, 1936), 350, 354; Pitkin, *Statistical View*, 53-54, 119-20, 125-26.

TABLE I—*Quarterly and Year-End Prices on*

Security	Jan. 5, 1807	April 29, 1807	July 17, 1807	Oct. 11, 1807	Dec. 3, 1807
U.S. Gov. 6% Certificates	99	98½	98½	98½	98½
U.S. Gov. 3% Certificates	61	64	63	64	64
U.S. Gov. 8% Certificates	103½	102½	101½	102½	102¼
Bank of the United States	134	127	127	123	123
Bank of Pennsylvania	136	134	134	133	133½
Bank of North America	145	142	140	145	145
Bank of Philadelphia	125	128	125½	122½	124
Water Loan	PAR	101	102	NQ†	103
Schuylkill Bridge	70	65	70	70	70
Delaware Bridge	UNC‡	70	UNC	NQ	UNC
Lancaster Turnpike	77½	88½	85	95	93

Security	Jan. 16, 1808	April 12, 1808	July 13, 1808	Oct. 23, 1808	Dec. 23, 1808
U.S. Gov. 6% Certificates	98	99	102	102	103
U.S. Gov. 3% Certificates	64	64	64½	65	67
U.S. Gov. 8% Certificates	101½	101	103½	101	101½
Bank of the United States	118	118	124	130	132
Bank of Pennsylvania	130	136	142½	145	150
Bank of North America	140	140	143	145	150
Bank of Philadelphia	121½	122	NQ	128	136
Water Loan	101	103	104	104	104
Schuylkill Bridge	70	70	70	72½	72½
Delaware Bridge	UNC	79	PAR	79	PAR
Lancaster Turnpike	95	93¼	95	95	90

* Prices taken from Paulson's *American Daily Advertiser*
† No quotation

*the Philadelphia Stock Exchange, 1807-1810**

Security	Jan. 9, 1809	April 11, 1809	July 17, 1809	Oct. 12, 1809	Dec. 15, 1809
U.S. Gov. 6% Certificates	101½	102½	102	101½	103
U.S. Gov. 3% Certificates	64½	65	65	66	66
U.S. Gov. 8% Certificates	NQ	NQ	NQ	NQ	NQ
Bank of the United States	126	127½	825§	127	129
Bank of Pennsylvania	142	142	142	141	141
Bank of North America	149	147	147	150	150
Bank of Philadelphia	133	NQ	129½	133½	134
Water Loan	104	104	NQ	104	104
Schuylkill Bridge	75	72½	72	73	74
Delaware Bridge	PAR	PAR	PAR	PAR	PAR
Lancaster Turnpike	86	87½	83½	80	82

Security	Jan. 10, 1810	April 6, 1810	July 17, 1810	Oct. 5, 1810	Dec. 11, 1810
U.S. Gov. 6% Certificates	104	103½	103½	104	104
U.S. Gov. 3% Certificates	67	65½	64½	65	66
U.S. Gov. 8% Certificates	NQ	NQ	NQ	NQ	NQ
Bank of the United States	131	115	111	113	120
Bank of Pennsylvania	142	140	140	140½	140
Bank of North America	150	146	146	146	149
Bank of Philadelphia	136	137	133	132	135½
Water Loan	105	104	104	105	104
Schuylkill Bridge	75	75	75	75	75
Delaware Bridge	PAR	PAR	PAR	PAR	PAR
Lancaster Turnpike	85	87	87	88	90

‡ Listed "uncertain"
§ This figure is correctly transcribed. It is obviously a misprint.

tion's efforts at economic coercion. There are some indications that the volume of business done on the Philadelphia exchange varied with political events, but this did not affect the prices of stocks.[17] These figures show that while there was a sharp decline in the price of the most common commodities sold in Philadelphia immediately after the enactment of the embargo legislation, the economy adjusted quickly, reached or surpassed preembargo levels within a year, and did not react adversely to subsequent commercial restrictions.

Less systematic, but no less accurate information, bears out this contention. Summarizing the information contained in his many charts, Pitkin asserts that prices for the most important products of the Middle Atlantic states actually increased after the embargo. Using Pitkin's figures and many that have come to light since, Norman Risjord shows that the value of these products nearly doubled in 1810 and 1811.[18]

The account books in the Denny-O'Hara papers show that the volume of business grew constantly. From the fall of 1807 to the outbreak of the war the number of sales and the variety of products sold increased steadily. Particularly interesting is the increasing volume in such items as cloth, gloves, stockings, ladies' gloves, silk, silk ribbons, and buttons. This would imply that the people in the Pittsburgh area had the money with which to buy these items which, at the time, were considered luxury items. The constantly rising volume of wood, nails, tools, and farm implements indicates that there was a growing amount of building and improvement. At the same time,

[17] For comments on the business done on the exchange, see Vaux to Jonathan Thompson, Oct. 15, 1811, Thompson Collection, Historical Society of Pennsylvania; John Cox to Vaux, Aug. 28, 1811, Vaux Papers, Historical Society of Pennsylvania.

[18] Pitkin, *Statistical View*, 95, 105, 119-20, 125-26, 128-31. Norman K. Risjord, "1812: Conservatives, War-Hawks and the Nation's Honor," *William and Mary Quarterly*, 3d series, XVIII (April, 1961), 204.

prices remained relatively stable. Three pairs of plain gloves cost $3.37½ on April 8, 1810; one pair of gloves was sold for $1.15 in January 1814. On July 7, 1810, one scrubbing bucket and one scrubbing brush cost $1.81. The price was the same in February 1813. A scrubbing brush alone was $0.50 in April 1810; $0.52 in May 1814. The price of cloth varies from a low of $0.87½ for a quarter yard in April 1810, to a high of $1.27 a quarter yard in June 1811. But the entries in the account books do not indicate the type of cloth involved in these transactions, and the difference in prices probably indicates a difference in quality rather than higher prices for cloth. For example, the account of Peter Colt carries a sale of a quarter yard of cloth at $0.91 on April 2, 1810, and a sale of one yard at $4.22 on April 13, 1810. Whiskey remained at a steady $0.40 per gallon from 1807 to 1813.

The account books show that most transactions were cash and that all accounts were usually paid in full. The managers made some loans to cover purchases, but these were small loans to established customers and were always paid promptly.[19] The Daybook of Beeson's Store in Pittsburgh also indicates a lively and profitable business. The very fact that it opened and prospered after the passage of the embargo is a strong indication that economic conditions were generally good.[20] Another general store prospered in Pittsburgh, but complete records are not available before 1813. It is known that it was in operation in 1808 and there is no reason to doubt that it was prosperous before the war.[21]

The newspapers of western Pennsylvania carry numerous advertisements of new stores opening and soliciting

---

[19] Denny-O'Hara account book, 1807 to 1812, Denny-O'Hara Papers.
[20] Daybook of Beeson's Store, Armour Collections, Western Pennsylvania Historical Society.
[21] Dunbar Furnace Daybook, Armour Collection, Western Pennsylvania Historical Society.

business. All promise to pay high prices and to sell at reasonable rates. In 1811 and 1812 many of these advertisements state that the stores would sell only goods of domestic manufactures thereby "satisfying the wishes of patriots" and "encouraging such manufactories by providing an outlet for their goods." The many notices of the opening of new iron foundries, nail factories, cotton mills, fulling and carding mills show that domestic manufacturing did increase after 1810.[22] The number of cotton spindles rose steadily from 160 in 1806 to 294 in 1810 and 822 in 1814.[23]

Cramer's Pittsburgh Almanac announced in 1807 that "the town is growing rapidly and prospering greatly," as can be seen in the erection of factories. "[It] has an extensive glass factory . . . a factory of cotton . . . an air furnace . . . several nail factories, two extensive breweries whose beer and porter is equal to that so much celebrated in London." Copper and tin factories, two rope walks, a paper factory and the first steam grist mill in the country would soon be added to the area's growing industrial base.[24] The next year Cramer promised that "we will see all heavy articles manufactured among ourselves. . . . There is at least $20,000 worth of hardware sold out of our stores which ought to be made on the spot." Other signs of growth to which he pointed with pride were building statistics. These facts, indicate a rather steady rate of economic development which could not occur during a period of depression. A similar conclusion can be reached from figures describing the economic conditions in central and eastern Pennsylvania.

[22] See Washington *Reporter*, July 11, Sept. 14, Nov. 5, Nov. 12, Dec. 10, 1811, Jan. 27, 1812; Pittsburgh *Commonwealth*, Feb. 7, Feb. 28, March 7, April 21, June 16, July 14, 1811, Feb. 15, 1812.

[23] J. N. Boucher, *A Century and a Half of Pittsburgh and Her People* (New York, 1908).

[24] *Cramer's Pittsburgh Almanac*, 1808, p. 57.

John Kraus was a typical farmer in central Pennsylvania who left some revealing account books. His gross income rose from $1,441.80 in 1806 to $1,705.08 in 1809. The increase of $137.00 from 1807 to 1808 is the greatest annual increment. Some of the details of this account are very informative. In 1806 Kraus earned $88.14 for marketing grain. In 1807 sale of grain earned $94.17, rising to $99.26 in 1808 and $103.04 in 1809. The account books do not tell how much or what kind of grain was sold, but the figures show that there was a profitable market. Kraus also earned money by carding wool and selling cotton and wool and yarn, with an annual increase in profit. A sign of his prosperity is the fact that he borrowed sums of money every year except 1807, generally using the money for improvements or equipment. In 1809 he bought an additional 15 acres increasing the size of his farm from 75 to 90 acres.[25]

Figures found in county histories further strengthen the impression of economic prosperity. Between 1800 and 1810 the area of cleared land in Somerset County grew from 27,756 to 48,874 acres. The number of cabins increased from 836 to 901, while the number of houses grew from 413 to 499. There was a marked increase in the number of gristmills, sawmills, and fulling and carding mills, as well as an increase in the amount of livestock.[26] Figures for Bradford County indicate similar conditions.[27] In Delaware County in eastern Pennsylvania farmers had many incentives "to improve their lands and thereby increase their products" in the prewar period. "The people [of our county] were in a prosperous condition." Farmers found ready markets for their crops, and "many new mills

[25] The account book for 1809 is published in the *Perkiomen Region,* XII (April 1934), 84-88.
[26] William H. Koontz, *History of Bradford and Somerset Counties, Pennsylvania,* 3 vols. (New York, 1906), II, 176-78.
[27] Ibid., 184-89.

were established and profited greatly by . . . the demands
of the citizens in Philadelphia and other places."[28]   Other
county histories provide similar examples of prosperity
for farmers.[29]   The standard history of Philadelphia comments that "everywhere in Philadelphia the germs of great
industrial enterprise were taking root. . . . Philadelphia
was becoming an industrial and commercial metropolis."[30]
Reporting on his visit to Philadelphia in 1806 John Melish
said he was impressed with the importance of manufacturing in the city and its overall prosperous appearance. When he returned in 1811 he was impressed by the
rapid progress the city had made. "Many new important
manufactures had been established and flourished in an
eminent degree."[31]   In 1811 he reported from Pittsburgh
that manufactures were as well established as in the eastern parts of the state. He estimated the manufactures of
Pittsburgh at more than $1 million annually. This, he
calculated, resulted in "a capital accumulation of $700,000
annually to be invested [in] further expansion of manufacturing."[32]   The correspondence of Matthew Carey, noted
Philadelphia bookseller, contained many complaints that
"the sale of books is so bad we can scarcely muster as much

[28] George Smith, *History of Delaware County, Pennsylvania* (Philadelphia, 1862), 351-53.

[29] See, for example, I. H. M'Cauley, *Historical Sketch of Franklin
County, Pennsylvania* (Chambersburg, 1878); Samuel E. Bates, *History
of Erie County* (Chicago, 1884); Joseph Bausman, *History of Beaver
County, Pennsylvania* (New York, 1904); Alfred Creigh, *History of
Washington County* (Harrisburg, 1871); William H. Egle, *History of the
Counties of Dauphin and Lebanon in the Commonwealth of Pennsylvania*
(Philadelphia, 1883).

[30] John Scharf and Thomas Westcott, *History of Philadelphia,* 3 vols.
(Philadelphia, 1884), I, 510-36.

[31] John Melish, *Travels Through the United States of North America
in the Years 1806 and 1807, and 1809, 1810, and 1811,* 2 vols. (Philadelphia, 1815), I, 153, II, 3.

[32] Ibid., II, 55-57. Alexander and Phillips to Carey, Aug. 9, 1808,
Lea and Febiger Collection, Pennsylvania Historical Society. See also
Carey's account books in the same collection.

money as will pay our paperman." But the account books indicate a different situation. Each year Matthew Carey published an increasing number of books and pamphlets which he sold all over the country, and each year he made substantial profits.

The economic posture and activity of the state government and the comments of political leaders provide more evidence which deny depression. Every year from 1805 to 1814 the state had a handsome surplus (see table II). • During this decade expenditures were rising annually, and the surplus indicates that the state's income was rising more rapidly than its expenditures. By far the largest source of income was from sale of lands, not only indicating that land was available, but that it was desirable.

The messages of the governors also paint pictures of prosperity. In December 1805 McKean informed the legislature that "the prosperity of Pennsylvania conspicuously displays the industry . . . of her citizens and surpasses the most ardent expectations" of the government and the people. The following year, he repeated this sentiment in his message. The legislature expressed gratification at the image of prosperity which the governor had represented, taking it as "proof . . . of the policies of the government . . . and the benefits of republican institutions." The years after 1808 were also prosperous ones for the state.[33] In his first annual message the newly elected governor, Simon Snyder, congratulated the state on its prosperity. Remarking favorably on the increase in construction, the large increase in cleared acreage, and the progress being made in bridge and turnpike construction, he placed particular emphasis on the development of manufactures.

[33] Higginbotham, *Keystone,* 220.

TABLE II—*State Income and Expenditure, 1805-1812*

Year	Receipts	Expenditure	Surplus
1805	369,522.61	229,582.30	139,940.31
1806	380,549.49	309,826.01	70,723.48
1807	327,367.17	236,071.94	91,295.23
1808	341,735.95	295,495.39	46,239.56
1809	594,190.05	312,139.95	282,050.10
1810	636,015.18	594,389.78	41,625.40
1811	449,935.15	389,889.22	60,045.93
1812	498,959.75	308,960.74	189,998.91

MAJOR SOURCES OF INCOME			
Year	Land Sales	Tavern Licenses	Duties on Sales at Auction
1805	63,712.46	21,003.60	18,349.21
1806	66,140.02	21,645.72	26,689.24
1807	47,243.92	15,118.28	17,602.62
1808	40,009.26	——	29,882.64
1809	318,129.49	——	33,635.22
1810	93,644.42	29,373.49	53,706.67
1811	137,235.82	29,515.46	54,045.45
1812	125,125.28	26,417.76	55.713.91*

MAJOR EXPENDITURES			
Year	Government Expenses	Militia, Arms, and Ordnance	Special Appropriations‡
1805	141,066.62	13,348.74	14,000.00
1806	140,530.34	14,497.75	124,401.36
1807	152,816.59	7,966.39	18,483.46
1808	Figures are not available for this year		
1809	149,282.02	11,883.60	82,544.15
1810	130,774.15	8,916.62†	——
1811	155,196.26	7,300.21†	164,171.21
1812	162,646.32	10,223.84†	71,229.26

Our mills and furnaces are greatly multiplied; new beds of ore have been discovered, and the industry and enterprise of our citizens are turning them to the most useful purposes. Many new and highly valuable manufactories have been established, and we now make in Pennsylvania, various articles of domestic use for which, two years since, we were wholly dependent upon foreign nations.

We have lately had established in Philadelphia large shot manufactories; floor-cloth manufactories; and a queensware pottery, upon an extensive scale. These are all in successful operation, independent of immense quantities of cotton and wool, flax and hemp, leather and iron, which are annually manufactured in our state.[34]

In his next message, Snyder informed the legislature that the state "continued to prosper" despite the oppressive orders of Great Britain and France and the commercial restrictions of the federal government. He suggested to the legislature that our dependence on Great Britain for manufactured goods lay at the root of the nation's problems and proposed that the legislature pass laws to encourage domestic manufactures. Every opening message included similar statements congratulating the

[34] *Pennsylvania Archives*, 4th series, IV, 677.

NOTES FOR TABLE II

* This surplus was pledged for building ships to be turned over to the national government.

† Expenditures followed by this sign are for militia exclusively.

‡ The special appropriation of 1809 was "for purchase of stock." There is no indication of what stock. The special appropriation for 1811 is for "improvements and purchase of stock." The special appropriation for 1812 is divided as follows: $38,461.00 for improvements and $32,768.26 for "expenses consequent to the declaration of war." (These figures are compiled from the annual reports of the state treasurer and state auditor which can be found as appendixes to the *Senate Journal* for the appropriate year.)

state on its prosperity, and the care the legislature had taken to foster manufacturing.[35]

In letters to his brother, Matthew, Jonathan Roberts, a member of the Pennsylvania House of Representatives, often expressed satisfaction at the state's economic growth and surprise that the commercial legislation passed by Congress did not hinder it. His later letters indicate that he believed the embargo had helped by forcing the United States to build up its productive capacity.[36] Thomas Rogers told Roberts that in spite of their defeat in the congressional elections, Federalist farmers were content because of the high price of wheat.[37] William Findley received information from Manuel Eyre expressing satisfaction at his own and his friends' prosperity. He hoped that something could be done for the commercial interests so they could share in the prosperity.[38] On the eve of the war Stephen Girard wrote to one of his captains, "New manufactures are establishing daily and making great progress." If the trend continues "there will be little demand for foreign merchandise."[39]

The figures of manufacturing and internal improvement companies chartered by the state are another indication that money was available and that people were willing to invest their capital in commercial enterprises (see table III).

All of these facts indicate that Pennsylvania, unlike the West and South, did not suffer an economic depression

[35] *Pennsylvania House Journal*, 16th sess., 1805-1806, pp. 14-15, 17th sess., 1806-1807, p. 18, 19th sess., 1808-1809, pp. 23-24; *Pennsylvania Archives*, 4th series, IV, 671-73.

[36] Jonathan Roberts to Matthew Roberts, March 7, May 19, 1808, Jan. 14, 1810, July 6, 1811, Roberts Papers.

[37] Rogers to Jonathan Roberts, Oct. 1, 1812, Roberts Papers.

[38] Eyre to Findley, Jan. 12, 1812, Gallatin Papers, New York Historical Society.

[39] Stephen Girard's Letter Book #13, Letter #81, Stephen Girard Papers, American Philosophical Society, Philadelphia.

TABLE III—*Commercial Charters Granted by Pennsylvania, 1805-1812*

Year	No. of Companies Chartered	No. of Shares Authorized	No. of Shares Sold	No. of Buyers
INTERNAL IMPROVEMENTS COMPANIES				
1805	2	900	805	140
1806	1	600	600	54
1807	1	700	613	182
1808	7	4,100	3,997	1,502
1809	1	250	201	47
1810	3	2,000	1,274	290
1811	11	6,000	5,768	1,985
1812	6	3,100	3,093½	644
MANUFACTURING COMPANIES				
1807	2	500	500	14
1808	4	800	800	11
1809	9	1,750	1,750	37
1810	11	1,600	1,600	28
1811	14	2,100	2,100	31
1812	29	3,400	3,400	47

In most cases buyers bought two or three shares. Twenty shares is the other most common figure. In one case there was a buyer who bought seventy-one shares, another one bought forty shares; these were the two largest single blocks sold. In every case in which an internal improvement company did not sell the number of shares it was authorized to sell, the state bought the unsold number at par value. (Figures compiled from *Pennsylvania Archives,* 9th series, IV, V, VI.)

in the period following the embargo. However valid the Taylor-Latimer hypothesis may be for the Mississippi Valley and the South, it does not explain western Pennsylvania's support for the war. The application of this hypothesis to the entire state is quite unwarranted.

Most of the West's economic problems resulted from certain peculiar characteristics of its economy, and as Taylor himself states, "the bubble of 1805 would soon have burst . . . even without the embargo and non-intercourse" from the "underlying weaknesses in the immediate situation."[40]

The economy of the Mississippi Valley was not at all integrated. The area could not possibly consume all the agricultural goods it produced; it could not manufacture the most essential tools or other finished goods its farmers needed. It depended almost entirely on foreign markets to dispose of its own production and had to import virtually all of its manufactured goods. This, as Taylor shows, made the area prey to every shift in the foreign policy of either belligerent, or of the national government. Since the only reasonable port of exit was New Orleans, it gave dealers there a stranglehold on the entire valley's economy which they used with great advantage to themselves, especially when temporary, local conditions created a glut on the market. The South had to contend with all of these problems, as well as those created by the one-crop nature of its agriculture.

Pennsylvania farmers did not have to contend with any of these problems. Virtually no part of western Pennsylvania's prosperity depended on foreign commerce. The rapid progress of manufacturing in that state created local centers of industry which consumed virtually all the locally produced agricultural goods and manufactured not only the basic necessities, but even some of the luxuries. Farmers in western Pennsylvania found a ready outlet for their goods in Pittsburgh. In 1815, Pittsburgh breweries alone consumed from twenty to thirty thousand bushels of grain. From the steady increase in the number of gristmills, it can be assumed that production of grain and meal also increased. *Cramer's Pittsburgh Almanac* states that "much whiskey was produced" providing another outlet for Pennsylvania farmers. Bacon and ham

[40] Taylor, "Agrarian Discontent," *Journal of Political Economy* (August, 1931), 474.

were also produced in "large quantities." This would indicate that there was significant hog production, providing yet another outlet for grains. In 1810 Pittsburgh had two glass factories, two cotton mills, a button factory, an iron grinding mill, and forty-four weaving looms.[41]

These factories produced almost all the manufactured goods needed in the area, and shipped large quantities of manufactured goods to Ohio, Kentucky, and Tennessee. Wilson estimated that in addition to the $1 million profit which Pittsburgh's manufacturing enterprises netted, transportation enterprises and its location as the gateway to the northwest produced another $1 million.[42] Trade with the upper Mississippi Valley was another lucrative source of income.

What was true of Pittsburgh, was even more true of Philadelphia. Victor Clark places Philadelphia second only to New York in industrial development in 1810. Balthasar Meyer states that Philadelphia and Baltimore provided an accessible domestic market for all the agricultural staples produced north of the Potomac and east of the Appalachians.[43]

The manufacturing census of 1810 showed Pennsylvania leading the Union in the quantity and diversity of industrial products, with the heaviest concentration in the Philadelphia area.[44] That census estimates the state's production at $33,691,676—slightly more than 19 percent of the national total. At the same time, commercial interests in the state were declining slowly. In 1789 Pennsylvania provided 20 percent of the nation's tonnage

[41] Cramer's Pittsburgh Almanac, 1809, pp. 34-38; 1810, pp. 52-58; Wilson, Pittsburgh, 148; Riddle, Pittsburgh Directory, 140; Catherine Reiser, Pittsburgh's Commercial Development (Harrisburg, 1951), 11-16.

[42] Wilson, Pittsburgh, 152-59.

[43] Victor Clark, History of Manufacturers in the United States 1807-1860 (Washington, 1916), 428; Balthasar Meyer, History of Transportation (Washington, 1917), 572.

[44] American State Papers: Finance, II, 746-63.

in foreign trade; by 1816, the figure had dropped to less than 10 percent indicating further that conditions in the export market were of little concern to Pennsylvanians. Thus, it was not the dictates of economy that led to the Pennsylvanians' decision to support the war.

CHAPTER THREE

The Nation's Honor
and the Party's Welfare

Bradford Perkins, Roger Brown, Reginald Horsman, and Norman Risjord contend that the sectional and economic interpretations of the causes of the War of 1812 associated with Julius Pratt and George Taylor contain unproved assertions and irreconcilable internal inconsistencies. However accurately these theories might explain the motives of the West or the South, most recent historians assert that they cannot be extended to explain the sizable war vote of the Middle Atlantic states. In an effort to explain why the nation as a whole went to war, rather than any particular section, recent historians have sought a broad, unifying factor, which could explain the vote of all sections. This search has brought them full circle to a reemphasis on diplomatic relations and maritime grievances. Without denying that other factors were present, these historians generally accept the proposition that "the only unifying factor, present in all sections of the country, was the growing feeling of patriotism, the realization that something must be done to vindicate the national honor."[1]

In spite of subtle differences among themselves as to which maritime and diplomatic factors were most important, and why they reached a climax in the summer of

1812, there is general agreement that Americans genuinely felt that "national honor was suffering from British action at sea."[2]

A search through the correspondence, newspapers, speeches, and works of the period shows that considerations of national honor, prompted by the nation's diplomatic and maritime experience from 1807 to 1812, convinced many Pennsylvanians that war was necessary.

The people of Pennsylvania and their representatives wanted to avert war. They supported every measure of commercial coercion, commended every effort to negotiate a settlement, and accepted gratefully every temporary relaxation of tensions, hoping it would become permanent. When commercial coercion failed, when negotiations proved futile and tensions continued to mount, Pennsylvanians gradually accepted the necessity of defending the nation's rights by force of arms.

Pennsylvanians who wrote about the war shortly after its close strongly support this contention. Describing the mood of congressional Republicans at the opening of the Twelfth Congress, Jonathan Roberts recorded in his memoirs, "we met under a decided impression that if negotiation further failed, War must be declared. Embargo and non-intercourse had been tried and failed, no other honorable course seemed open."[3] Charles Ingersoll, a prominent Philadelphia Republican and wartime con-

[1] Norman K. Risjord, "1812: Conservatives, War-Hawks and the Nation's Honor," *William and Mary Quarterly*, 3d series, XVIII (April, 1961), 204. For other recent studies stressing maritime causes and national honor see A. L. Burt, *The United States, Great Britain, and British North America* (New York, 1961); Bradford Perkins, *Prologue to War: England and the United States, 1805-1812* (Berkeley, 1961); Roger H. Brown, *The Republic in Peril: 1812* (New York, 1964); and Reginald Horsman, *The Causes of the War of 1812* (Philadelphia, 1962).

[2] Reginald Horsman, "Western War Aims, 1811-1812," *Indiana Magazine of History*, LIII (January, 1957), 9.

[3] Philip S. Klein, "Memoirs of Senator Jonathan Roberts," *Pennsylvania Magazine of History and Biography*, LXI (1938), 446-47.

gressman, often referred to the War of 1812 as the Second War for Independence. Britain's policy "had brought the existence of the United States as an independent nation into question." After all peaceful efforts had failed to win recognition of our rights, war was the only recourse.[4] Henry Brackenridge, a leader of the Republican party in Pittsburgh, characterized Britain's policy as "illegal and insulting" and concluded that "nothing was to be expected from any . . . arrangement on the part of our enemy; that nothing short of a change in her general policy would suffice and nothing but a war could effect this change."[5]

Most of the Pennsylvania congressmen who voted for war had sat in earlier sessions and had supported the more pacific methods of commercial retaliation. Their conversion in the spring of 1812 reflects a gradual change in the opinion of their constituents, brought about by the realization that the efforts to preserve our rights by methods short of war had failed; that only two alternatives remained to the nation: war and national honor, or continued peace and national humiliation. What happened in the five years from 1807 to 1812 to create this state of mind?

The military stalemate in Europe led each of the belligerents to intensify its efforts to fight the war by restricting the commerce of the other. The British orders-in-council and the French decrees made practically all United States shipping subject to seizure and confiscation by Great Britain or France.

The initial response of the American government was to protest violations of American rights and to appeal to both belligerents for redress of grievances. The appeal

[4] Charles Ingersoll, *Historical Sketch of the Second War Between the United States and Great Britain* (Philadelphia, 1845), 41; see also William Meigs, *The Life of Charles J. Ingersoll* (Philadelphia, 1897), 68.
[5] H. M. Brackenridge, *History of the Late War Between the United States and Great Britain* (Philadelphia, 1844), 50.

proved ineffective and by 1806 the administration decided on more direct methods. Senator Andrew Gregg of Pennsylvania introduced a stringent nonimportation measure which would prohibit the importation of most goods from Europe. After long debate and serious divisions among congressional Republicans, a much more limited nonimportation measure was passed. Gregg opposed the emasculation of his bill on the grounds that strong measures would show American determination better than half measures and might force the belligerents, especially Britain, to respect American rights. This was the first step in the American effort to use economic pressure against the European belligerents.[6] Neither belligerent was willing to yield, a major incident seemed inevitable, and finally occurred on June 22, 1807, when the H.M.S. *Leopard* fired on the U.S.S. *Chesapeake* in American waters, boarded her, and took off four men alleged to be British deserters.

Many Americans considered the *Chesapeake* incident a more serious offense than impressment from merchant vessels or interference with American commerce. They saw in it the culmination of years of Anglo-American disagreement, a direct attack on the nation's sovereignty, and demanded that the government take vigorous action to defend the nation's rights.

According to William Duane, editor of the *Aurora*, the *Chesapeake* affair was not an accident, but a premeditated hostile act indicating complete disregard not only of our neutral rights, but of our national honor and independence. He told his readers that they were already involved in war, and that it did not begin with the *Chesapeake* incident. It was but the "last outrage" in a series which

[6] *Annals of Congress*, 9th Cong., 10th sess., 771-72; Herbert Heaton, "Non-Importation, 1806-1812," *Journal of Economic History*, I (November, 1941), 178-98; Brown, *The Republic in Peril*, 17-19.

began in 1793. From that time, at least, Britain's policy had been marked by a determined effort to wreck our commerce, to deprive us of our territory, and to destroy our independence. During this whole period our government had followed a commendable policy of neutrality and forbearance but "to submit longer . . . will be but sinking ourselves in disgrace and inviting the scorn and degradation of the power that has assailed us." The American people, Duane urged, must suppress party feelings and "pledge support to the administration in whatever method it should choose to assert our rights, defend our independence, and redeem our honor."[7]

Duane demanded a special session of Congress to which he recommended a "total suspension of intercourse" as the only measure which "will secure the American people from national disgrace and personal plunder." Such a measure would be effective enough to reduce the British to terms within six months. If the United States did not take this, or similar vigorous action, the country "should proclaim to the world that the liberty with which . . . the toils of our fathers made us free [is] not worth defending or enjoying."[8]

The citizens of Philadelphia agreed with Duane. A public meeting, attended by more than six thousand people, unanimously approved resolutions condemning "the outrage" committed by the *Leopard,* calling it "an act of such consummate violence and wrong, and of so barbarous and murderous a character, that it would debase and degrade any nation . . . to submit to it."[9] The Federalist Pennsylvania *Gazette* also reported this meeting and approved of its resolutions. The British, it suggested, may be justified in retrieving deserters from

[7] Philadelphia *Aurora,* June 30, July 7, 1807.
[8] Ibid., June 29, 1807, Jan. 6, 1808.
[9] Ibid., July 7, 1807.

American merchant vessels, but nothing can justify "the insult to our sovereignty" implicit in an attack on a military vessel. Zachariah Paulson referred to the incident as an "unexampled outrage" which "tells us that we have a second Independence to gain from Great Britain." He, too, reported and approved of the public meetings.[10]

Both Republican and Federalist papers were particularly impressed by the nonpartisan character of the meeting. Noting that the chairman was a Republican and the secretary a Federalist, both editors praised everyone for suppressing party differences to "the needs of the nation's honor" and promised to support any administration effort to "avenge this outrage." Michael Leib, who became one of the leaders of the antiadministration Republicans, and an opponent of the war, described the meeting as a sight "which the Gods themselves might have looked down on with delight." The Federalists, he wrote, asked to participate in the sponsorship of the meeting, "that it might evince to the world the perfect accordance of the public in reprobation of british [sic] outrage. . . . Distinction of sect seemed to be forgotten in national feeling and support of the administration."[11]

The Carlisle *Gazette* reported similar nonpartisan meetings in central Pennsylvania. Two sets of resolutions reported on July 10 were exactly the same as those adopted at the Philadelphia meeting. Other meetings expressed similar sentiments and pledged the people "to make any sacrifices and endure any hazards to which the quest for retribution would lead." The editor praised "the patriotism, loyalty and energy" of the citizens, "with whose sentiments we heartily agree."

[10] Pennsylvania *Gazette*, July 9, 1807; *Paulson's American Daily Advertiser*, July 1, 1807.

[11] Philadelphia *Aurora*, June 29, June 30, July 2, July 3, July 4, 1807; Pennsylvania *Gazette*, July 2, July 9, 1807; Michael Leib to C. H. Rodney, July 2, 1807, Gratz Collection, Historical Society of Pennsylvania.

One correspondent minced no words. The attack on the *Chesapeake* was absolute proof "of the determination of the British to dragoon us into submission." He demanded resolute action by the government, and if that failed to secure the people's rights, he wanted war. Toasts drunk at Fourth of July celebrations reveal a similar temper. They invariably condemn the British and the attack on the *Chesapeake* and then point to the "heroes of '76" as examples of the energy "with which threats to our independence must be met." Like their forefathers, the celebrants pledged their "lives . . . fortunes . . . and sacred honor" to defend the independence they had won.[12] Editorially, the *Gazette* called for "coercive measures stronger than mere remonstrance," and for war if these did not secure their rights.[13] The Dauphin *Guardian* also carried reports of protest meetings throughout Dauphin County. Many of these urge immediate and forceful retaliation and pledge to support the administration in any action it might take to "avenge" this outrage. "A citizen" warned that if measures of retaliation were not taken immediately, "America had better at once deliver up her independence." The Federalist Harrisburg *Times* also referred to the incident as an "outrage" but warned against making it a cause for war. Citing London newspapers and parliamentary debates to show that there were many in Britain who were shocked by the *Leopard*'s actions, the editor David Wright assured his readers that Britain would admit her error and be willing to make amends.

The same attitude appeared in the press in western Pennsylvania. The Pittsburgh *Commonwealth* described the incident as "a violent and unjustifiable insult upon

[12] Carlisle *Gazette*, July 3, July 10, July 17, July 24, 1807.

[13] Carlisle *Gazette*, July 10, July 17, 1807; Dauphin *Guardian*, July 7, July 14, July 21, 1807; Harrisburg *Times*, Sept. 21, 1807.

the dignity and honor of the country." The Washington *Reporter* called it an "outrage" and an "insult." The Federalist *Gazette* saw in it "a threat to our independence" and demanded "immediate apology and reparation." It joined the Republican papers in praising the nonpartisan composition of protest meetings, and advised that "domestic divisions must be submerged when the existence of the nation is at stake." The editor pledged his life and fortune "in support of any action" taken by the government "to prevent further insults."[14]

Pennsylvania politicians echoed these sentiments. After a reading of the Declaration of Independence, the General Assembly unanimously resolved "to die free men rather than submit to become vassals of Great Britain," and warned that "the cup of injury might be made to overflow." It praised the pacific efforts of the past and pledged itself to "sustain the measures of the general government . . . at the hazard of everything dear and valuable to men." The governor told the legislature that the attack on the *Chesapeake* had excited "public sensibility beyond forbearance" and left them "no alternative but war or degradation" if Britain did not repudiate the action and make adequate reparations. The General Assembly approved of these sentiments and expressed its complete confidence in the administration. If the measures taken by the federal government did not secure the rights of the United States, they agreed that the honor and safety of the county left no alternative but war.[15]

In Washington, John Smilie asserted that "wherever our armed ships are, there is our jurisdiction." Any attack on them is a direct attack on the United States which

[14] Pittsburgh *Commonwealth,* July 8, July 29, Aug. 4, Aug. 12, 1807; Washington *Reporter,* July 14, July 21, Aug. 4, Aug. 11, 1807; Pittsburgh *Gazette,* July 7, July 14, 1807.
[15] *Pennsylvania Senate Journal,* 1807-1808, pp. 53, 82-83, 89-91, 119; *Pennsylvania House Journal,* 1807-1808, p. 73.

requires immediate retaliation.[16] In a heavy "I-told-you-so" tone, Andrew Gregg wrote William Jones that if his stringent nonimportant measure had been adopted and enforced the tragedy might have been averted. When he heard of the incident, he "took it for granted that Congress would be called for the purpose of adopting some retaliatory measures. . . . That sentiment was general. All parties . . . seemed to be united in a spirit of resistance." He did not want war, but hoped that effective commercial legislation would be passed.[17]

More than any other previous incident, the attack on the *Chesapeake* roused the anger of the American people, and convinced them that measures stronger than remonstrance and protest were necessary if the United States were to win respect for its rights from the European belligerents. They did not insist upon immediate hostilities, but they did demand more direct and forceful action.

As a first step, Jefferson ordered all British warships from American waters.[18] The Pennsylvania press approved of this action as a precautionary measure, to be followed by more forceful action when Congress convened. "The course pursued is as vigorous as ought to have been expected," argued the Carlisle *Gazette*. Those who condemned the action as too weak were themselves "rash and precipitate." True, the attack on the *Chesapeake* was an act of war and it could have been construed as such and acted on accordingly, but it was not advantageous to do so. "It is the interest of the people and therefore the duty of the government to avert so great a calamity as war." The president's action adequately asserted American rights and would prevent similar incidents in the future, yet it left the door open for explanation and reparation. If the British failed to make proper satisfac-

16 *Annals of Congress*, 10th Cong., 1st sess., 811.
17 Gregg to Jones, Aug. 4, 1807, Jones Papers.
18 *American State Papers: Foreign Relations*, III, Nov. 19, 1807.

tion and give "acceptable assurances" for the future "more vigorous action can be taken later."[19]

By the time Congress convened in November 1807 England had not only failed to make reparation for the *Chesapeake* affair, but had continued her depredations on American commerce and her impressment of seamen from American ships. Transmitting documents showing the increased dangers to which American commerce was exposed "from the maritime pretensions of Great Britain and France," the president recommended to Congress adoption of an embargo as a protective measure for American shipping and as a retaliatory measure.[20] Four days later Congress passed the embargo act.[21]

At a public meeting in Philadelphia, William Jones praised the embargo as "a wise precaution" which protected United States ships and men against seizure and exerted enough pressure on the belligerents to ensure that they would soon be forced to respect United States rights. The meeting then passed resolutions approving the administration's efforts "to protect the nation's rights and preserve peace" and approved of the embargo as "an honorable alternative to war."[22]

On the whole, the people of Pennsylvania supported the policy of commercial restriction as an honorable alternative to war and as an effective weapon to secure their rights.[23] The mounting evidence in the succeeding years

[19] Carlisle *Gazette*, July 17, July 24, 1807. See also Philadelphia *Aurora*, July 16, July 21, July 23, 1807; Pittsburgh *Commonwealth*, July 18, July 25, Aug. 2, 1807; Washington *Reporter*, July 16, July 23, 1807; Dauphin *Guardian*, Aug. 2, Aug. 25, 1807, for similar statements.

[20] *American State Papers: Foreign Affairs*, III, 25.

[21] *Annals of Congress*, 10th Cong., 1st sess., 1222.

[22] Philadelphia *Aurora*, Oct. 3, 1808. Similar meetings and resolutions were reported in other parts of the state. See Pittsburgh *Commonwealth*, Oct. 7, Oct. 14, 1808; Carlisle *Gazette*, Sept. 19, Oct. 2, 1808; Washington *Reporter*, Sept. 14, Sept. 26, Oct. 6, 1808.

[23] Sanford Higginbotham, *Keystone of the Democratic Arch: Pennsylvania Politics, 1800-1816* (Harrisburg, 1952), 238.

that commercial restrictions were not achieving their intended goals, the growing hostility and intransigence of Great Britain, and the increasing difficulties which maintenance of the policy created for the Republican party disillusioned many Republicans. They had supported the system as an alternative to war but came to the conclusion that commercial measures were not enough; that war was the only solution to the nation's problems.

During the year that the embargo was in effect Pennsylvania Republicans supported it in the face of mounting Federalist opposition. It became the chief issue of the state elections of 1808. Federalists pointed to the measure as evidence of Republican subservience to France, and demanded a Federalist victory "to restore the *commercial habits* which have been unconstitutionally . . . infringed upon." A Federalist victory, they argued, would also restore prosperity "to our pauperized commonwealth."[24]

The election results indicated popular support for the • embargo. Republicans increased their majority in the state legislature and increased by one their domination of the state's congressional delegation. The Republican candidate for governor, Simon Snyder, who had lost the election of 1805 by five thousand votes to another Republican, won a resounding victory in 1808. He amassed the largest vote of any candidate for that office since 1790 and was the first Republican to carry Philadelphia since 1800.[25]

Of the four Pennsylvania congressmen who had voted against the embargo, three were reelected from traditionally Federalist districts. Of the four Republicans who had not voted on the embargo, three were defeated at the

24 Pennsylvania *Gazette,* Aug. 8, Aug. 15, 1808; Pittsburgh *Gazette,* Aug. 10, Sept. 7, 1808.
25 *Pennsylvania Manual,* 1953-1954, p. 91. Higginbotham, *Pennsylvania,* 174-75.

polls. The one who was reelected, Benjamin Say of Philadelphia, had been absent in the early part of the session, and his abstention was probably not taken as a sign of defection.

These heartening results and the seeming failure of negotiations made some Pennsylvania Republicans aggressive. In an effort to placate American sensibilities the British government had sent a special envoy, George Rose, to settle the affair. But his instructions were so narrow and his demands so great that the negotiations collapsed almost immediately.[26]

At the beginning of the discussions no one was very hopeful. Duane felt that England might be willing to settle the *Chesapeake* affair but that this would not be enough to warrant repeal of the embargo. Any settlement short of a complete recognition of our neutral rights and abandonment of impressment would only be temporary. "So long as Britain claims the right, whether she exercises it or not, our national honor and independence is not secure." He warned the people against allowing the negotiations to weaken their indignation. Britain had always followed the policy of committing an outrage, extending negotiations until passions cooled, and then refusing to make reparations. Other Republican newspapers in the state expressed the same sentiments.[27]

Andrew Gregg wrote William Jones that he did not believe George Rose would give adequate satisfaction, and hoped the administration would not be duped into accepting anything less than complete satisfaction.[28] John

[26] A good account of the Rose mission is available in Irving Brant, *James Madison: Secretary of State, 1808-1809* (Indianapolis, 1953), 409-18.

[27] Philadelphia *Aurora*, Feb. 2, Feb. 3, Feb. 5, March 7, 1808. See Carlisle *Gazette*, Feb. 5, Feb. 12, March 4, 1808; Pittsburgh *Commonwealth*, Feb. 13, Feb. 20, March 5, 1808.

[28] Gregg to Jones, Feb. 8, 1808, Jones Papers; see also William Findley to Joseph Hiester, April 9, 1808, Gregg Collection, Library of Congress.

Connelly and Jesse Higgins expressed similar sentiments in their letters to Jonathan Roberts, then a representative in the state legislature.[29] When the talks were discontinued in the spring and the *Chesapeake* affair remained unsettled, some Republicans began to demand measures more vigorous than embargo. Duane viewed the failure of the negotiations as evidence of Britain's disinclination to adjust relations between the two countries and, more ominously, of her unwillingness to accept the independence of the United States. If the embargo is not continued and "our rights are not vigorously asserted," he wrote, "the nation will revert to a position even lower than colonial dependence." Not only England, but other nations, will trample on our rights and "American independence will become a fiction."[30] William Jones regarded Rose's mission as "a temporizing maneuver" and its failure as a further example of "British arrogance." The attack on the *Chesapeake* was an act of war, and failure to respond to it as such had been read as a sign of weakness. He expressed faith in the embargo and demanded that it be continued until the end of the current session of Congress. He hoped that that body would use the time to prepare for war, and if American rights were still ignored when Congress adjourned, he favored an open declaration of war. He did not want war but believed it was "possible for a free, peaceful and virtuous people to prize the blessings of peace and depreciate the horrors of war [with] too much sensibility." Failure to act "after repeated insults" made Congress and supporters of the embargo "objects of derision." The failure of the Rose negotiations proved that the embargo was not a strong enough measure and more would be required "to protect the

29 Connelly to Roberts, March 1, 1808, Higgins to Roberts, Feb. 19, 1808, Roberts Papers.
30 Philadelphia *Aurora*, Feb. 26, March 3, March 4, 1808.

honor and independence of the country." Jones told a meeting called to protest New England opposition to the embargo that it had been intended only as a temporary measure which "must be superseded either by peaceful enjoyments of our rights and independence, or their maintenance at the point of the sword."[31]

In February and March all the Republican papers carried letters and editorials decrying the unwillingness of the British to settle the *Chesapeake* affair, warning that Britain would never grant us our rights until "we win them again on the field of battle" and urging the government to take vigorous action. Federalists blamed the failure of the negotiations on the intransigence of the administration.[32]

The Pennsylvania legislature, which had approved the embargo as "a wise pacific and patriotic measure calculated to exact . . . observance of our rights without resort to the horrors and dislocations of war" in its 1808 session, adopted in the following year a resolution pledging to support the government if war should become necessary to "protect our rights and defend our honor."[33]

In 1808 Governor McKean praised the "impartial, respectful and conciliatory" policy of the Federal government. The unwillingness to resort to war, even though there was adequate justification, would be a lesson to the world and would prove that republican governments can protect their rights by peaceful means.[34]

A year later Governor Snyder commended the "firmness and dignity" with which the administration "has sought . . . atonement for acknowledged injuries, and

[31] Jones to Macon, Nov. 16, 1808, Jones to Giles, Feb. 5, 1809, Jones Papers; Philadelphia *Aurora,* Jan. 18, Jan. 23, Jan. 25, 1809.
[32] Washington *Reporter,* Feb. 24, 1808; Harrisburg *Times,* Sept. 29, 1808.
[33] *Pennsylvania House Journal,* 1807-1808, p. 91, 1808-1809, pp. 14-16, 54-55.
[34] *Pennsylvania Archives,* 4th series, IV, 649-51.

security for unquestionable rights." Its efforts had been met "with indifference . . . or derision." He thought that now, however, "every candid mind . . . perceives that the independence of America must be maintained (as it was achieved) by the active patriotism and valor of her sons." No burden demanded by continued embargo or war could possibly compare "to the loss of national independence to be incurred by tame submission to the orders" of a European sovereign.[35]

In an effort to ease tensions, and perhaps hoping to buy time to allow the consolidation of opposition to the embargo, the British government appointed a new minister, David Erskine, to negotiate a settlement. Pennsylvania Republicans were not very optimistic. Duane contended that Britain had never consented to any concessions in the past, and there was no reason to believe that she would now. This was but another effort to lull the American people into forgetting an outrage without removing any grievances.[36] The Washington *Reporter* warned its readers not to expect too much from the negotiations. "Our honor will be redeemed on the field, not at the table," the editor told the readers. Jesse Higgins told Roberts that no one expected Erskine to make any new propositions and Jones informed Gregg that his hopes were not aroused.[37]

When the negotiations resulted in an acceptable agreement, the press grudgingly admitted that it had been wrong. The eastern press accepted the agreement, although Duane warned that it should not be considered permanent. Britain had been forced to make concessions for tactical reasons, he argued, and would revert to her old practices when the situation in Europe changed. The

[35] *Pennsylvania House Journal,* 1808-1809, pp. 19-22.
[36] Philadelphia *Aurora,* Aug. 22, Aug. 26, 1808.
[37] Washington *Reporter,* May 8, 1809; Higgins to Roberts, Dec. 14, 1808, Roberts Papers; Jones to Gregg, Jan. 14, 1809, Jones Papers.

Federalist papers saw the agreement as an admirable conversion in the Republican administration, and as evidence of a desire by the British to establish friendly relations. Jacob Elder, the editor of the *Guardian,* was elated at the agreement. He headlined the news, "REPUBLICAN TRIUMPH AND ENGLAND HUMBLED." The favorable agreement, he argued, was the result of the embargo and Republican "firmness."[38]

The western press did not accept the agreement quite so readily. The United States had given up too much and had received too little in return. Britain had not renounced its right to interfere with our trade, she had merely agreed to suspend the practice. Erskine had made no concessions on impressment, a practice "degrading to the honor of any independent nation that submits." When our "ardour to defend our rights" cools, Britain will forget the agreement and renew its violations.[39]

Britain's repudiation of the agreement killed whatever good feelings its negotiation had aroused and was seen as a further insult to our honor and as evidence that Britain could not be trusted. The appointment of Francis James "Copenhagen" Jackson to replace Erskine intensified the situation.[40] By refusing to ratify the treaty, Evans wrote, Britain has lost the confidence of all parties in the United States. They have now sent that villain Jackson who prepared the scaffold for innocent thousands at Copenhagen to America to practice infamy and fraud upon us."[41] Duane called the repudiation "an affront to

[38] Philadelphia *Aurora,* April 29, May 2, 1809; Carlisle *Gazette,* April 30, May 7, 1809; Pennsylvania *Gazette,* May 1, May 8, 1809; Dauphin *Guardian,* April 25, May 2, 1809.

[39] Washington *Reporter,* May 8, May 15, 1809; Pittsburgh *Commonwealth,* May 9, May 16, 1809; Carlisle *Gazette,* May 10, 1809.

[40] Jackson had delivered the ultimatum that preceded the bombardment of Copenhagen and the destruction of the Danish fleet. His appointment to the United States had been successfully opposed by Rufus King in 1801. See Perkins, *Prologue to War,* 220.

[41] Evans to Roberts, Aug. 3, 1809, Roberts Papers.

our honor"; the appointment of Jackson "an insult to our sensibilities." He began to advocate military preparations, the arming of merchant vessels, and if these measures failed, an outright declaration of war. Others were even more demanding. The repudiation of the Erskine agreement made an immediate declaration of war unavoidable "unless customary insult has rendered us callous to national honor."[42] The Washington *Reporter* concluded that neither negotiation nor commercial measures were adequate weapons with which to defend the nation's rights. "We ought either to resent our wrongs in a manly way, or cease to publish our disgraces. . . . Let us either behave like an independent people or lay aside their character [and] petition his sacred majesty, George III to restore [us] to the fold. Let us act the part of Americans or . . . Britains. Away with words, words, words, negotiations, and half-measures."[43]

Stating that "the conduct of Great Britain, and the insolence of her minister plenipotentiary, Francis J. Jackson, has produced a crisis that has excited publick feeling and anxiety to such an unexampled height that the representation of the freemen of the commonwealth cannot hesitate to accord with . . . the wishes of their constituents," the state legislature renewed its pledge to support whatever action the federal government intended to take and expressed "resentment against the government under whose orders the rights, dignity, and honor of the United States have been violated and insulted." The legislature pronounced "the violation on the part of Great Britain of a solemn agreement . . . to be . . . evidence of hostility and disregard for our rights."[44]

[42] Democratic *Press*, Aug. 16, 1809, cited in Higginbotham, *Pennsylvania*, 242.

[43] Philadelphia *Aurora*, May 4, July 21, Dec. 14, 1809; Washington *Reporter*, May 7, 1809.

[44] *Pennsylvania Senate Journal*, 1809-1810, pp. 104-105.

The governor called the conduct of Great Britain "a contemptuous disregard for solemnly and publicly plighted national honor which could not fail to arouse the resentment of the people . . . whose indignation has been greatly and justly heightened by the haughty and indecorous deportment of the present British minister." He regretted that the pacific measures of the administration had "not effected the object contemplated" but was grateful that they had excited "in every American's bosom, a fixed and determined resolution to support the general government in its patriotick efforts to maintain the honor, independence and just rights of our country."[45] He was so sure that repudiation of the Erskine agreement would lead to war that he ordered the adjutant general of the state militia to "do everything in [his] power to place the state of Pennsylvania in a situation to defend itself and contribute its full portion towards the defence of the just rights of the U. S." This order was sent because "the pleasing prospect of a Speedy and honorable adjustment of the disputes [had] vanished."[46]

The repudiation of the Erskine agreement and the appointment of Jackson did not bring war. Instead, there were continued efforts to win our rights by exertion of commercial pressure and negotiation. Nonintercourse followed embargo and was itself replaced by Macon's bill No. 2. Nothing seemed to help. Relations continued to deteriorate, and the anger of the people continued to mount.

Two events helped to clear the air. On May 16, 1811, John Rodgers, commander of the U.S.S. *President* overtook the H.M.S. *Little Belt,* forced her to strike her colors, and retrieved American sailors who had previously been impressed. Public reaction was immediate and favorable.

---

45 *Pennsylvania Senate Journal,* 1809-1810, pp. 10-12.
46 *Pennsylvania Archives,* 9th series, IV, 2733.

This was justified reprisal, but not provoked hostility. More such action would bring about a redress of our grievances much more readily than protest and ineffectual legislation. If England considered this attack an insult, it should note how often the United States has been insulted in a similar manner. America has tried embargo, nonintercourse, protest and negotiation, argument and threat, and has never retrieved one impressed seaman. "One fusillade has retrieved a dozen. Is there a lesson to be learned?" If the attack on the *Little Belt* gives England cause for war, how much more cause has that nation given the United States in the past five years?[47]

The incident momentarily changed relations between nations. The British demanded reparations from America, which had been denied satisfaction for the attack on the *Chesapeake* five years before, and could now say no. The administration could take a strong stand. "The *Little Belt-President* clash," in Perkins' words, "helped breed the psychological setting for war."[48]

Shortly before the *Little Belt* clash Napoleon seemingly repealed the French decrees insofar as they affected American commerce. Senator Gregg admitted that Napoleon's actions embarrassed the government because there "is some suspicion of her sincerity." However, he explained that many members of Congress believed that as a result Britain would repeal her orders. "But, if Britain fails . . . our government is pledged to put the non-intercourse system into operation."[49] Pursuant to the provisions of Macon's bill No. 2, President Madison opened trade with France, and imposed nonintercourse against

---

[47] Washington *Reporter*, June 3, June 10, 1811; Pittsburgh *Commonwealth*, June 4, June 11, 1811; Pittsburgh *Gazette*, June 4, 1811; Carlisle *Gazette*, June 4, 1811; Philadelphia *Aurora*, May 23, June 7, June 8, 1811; Harrisburg *Republican*, Dec. 31, 1811; Dauphin *Guardian*, June 4, July 6, 1811; Binns to Roberts, June 9, 1811, Jones Papers.

[48] Perkins, *Prologue to War*, 273.

[49] Gregg to Samuel Stewart, Feb. 23, 1811, Gregg Collection.

Great Britain. That nation rightly refused to believe that the French decrees had, in fact, been repealed, and refused to modify her orders in council which had allegedly been passed in retaliation against the French decrees. The impasse led to another round of negotiations between the United States and Great Britain.

Republicans in Pennsylvania insisted that the administration must make no concessions to Augustus J. Foster, the new British minister. They also accepted at face value, as did President Madison, Napoleon's assertion that the French decrees had been repealed. Why does Britain offer to adjust the *Chesapeake* affair just now, Rogers asked Congressman Roberts. Did Foster fear that the president might stir Congress to action and hope that this concession would dampen his ardor and the determination of Congress to demand recognition of all our rights? Did he hope to give the Federalists renewed hopes and new arguments "to prevent us from taking effective action to defend our honor?" "If they had really been anxious to do us justice they would have adjusted at least four years ago," and would return all American citizens on British ships, "a condition we must demand if we are to regain our lost honor." When Tripoli enslaved our sailors "we did not hesitate or negotiate; we should not now."[50]

Duane not only opposed concessions, he opposed even negotiation as a sign of weakness. The independence of the nation, he wrote, is not negotiable. "A nation which can tamely endure such aggressions as we have borne from Great Britain is not independent." Our ineffectual efforts to secure our rights by methods short of war "gave such a blow to our character . . . [that] the government has become an object of derision at home and abroad." Doubt had been cast on the "ability of Republican government to protect its citizens and property, and enforce its

[50] Rogers to Roberts, Nov. 17, 1811, Roberts Papers.

laws." Negotiations with Foster would be useless, Duane continued. The British minister came only because the reimposition of nonintercourse against Britain, consequent upon French repeal of her decrees, had disrupted Britain's economy. He did not come to make concessions, but to buy time for the British faction to sow dissention and force the administration to reopen trade with our enemy. This nation should expect no concessions from Britain and should not accept any. We should know from experience that Britain could not be trusted to keep her engagements. "Let him learn on this mission that the government can demand its rights . . . that the people have honor and pride . . . and are willing to defend them."[51]

Britain's failure to amend her orders-in-council following repeal of the French decrees provided another theme for the Republican press. Britain, the *Aurora* contended, had used the European war as an excuse to harass our commerce and threaten our independence because "she views us as her great rival in commerce and trade and considers every interest of her inhabitants centered in the destruction of our national independence."[52] Britain had justified her orders-in-council on the grounds of retaliation against French decrees. Now that the French had repealed their decrees, the British refused to repeal their orders. The real reason for the British orders was their fear of American growth in commerce and manufacture and their goal was to stop that growth before our competition became too serious.[53] A writer to the Pittsburgh *Commonwealth* concluded that from the debates in Parliament "it is apparent that Britain means to destroy

[51] Philadelphia *Aurora*, March 29, April 13, Aug. 2, 1811; Washington *Reporter*, April 15, April 22, May 5, May 19, 1811; Pittsburgh *Commonwealth*, April 7, April 21, May 4, May 18, 1811; Carlisle *Gazette*, April 17, May 14, 1811.
[52] Philadelphia *Aurora*, May 9, 1811.
[53] Carlisle *Gazette*, Aug. 23, 1811.

us."[54] In our effort to preserve the peace, the correspondent asserted, we had sacrificed the liberty and lives of our seamen, the property of our citizens, and had played into the hands of the British whose obvious goal was to destroy our commerce. "Worst of all our national honor is annihilated."[55]

In a widely reprinted letter a correspondent to the *Aurora* argued that repeal of the French decrees had made the decision for the United States. England's refusal to repeal its orders, he stated, proved that its aim was the destruction of America. He felt that independence, honor and patriotism demanded war.[56]

Pennsylvanians had obviously despaired of peaceful coercion. Many agreed with Duane that "we have received injuries the endurance of which has dishonored the national character which can now be retrieved only by recourse to arms."[57] With him, they looked to the Twelfth Congress, about to convene in Washington, for direction, and urged it to take effective action.

The Washington *Reporter* exhorted Congress to be done with "stratagems and tricks" which had gained the nation nothing but the odium of the world. The time had come when "we must give up our magnanimous policy" and take the "strong action necessary to preserve our honor, rights and independence." "Forbearance and conciliation have been carried by our government to their utmost limits," began an article in the Carlisle *Gazette*. "Every expedient compatible with the maintenance of our honor and independence has been resorted to. . . . Further forbearance can scarcely fail exposing us to the imputation

[54] Aug. 19, 1811.

[55] Philadelphia *Aurora*, Aug. 8, 1811.

[56] Philadelphia *Aurora*, Sept. 9, 1811; Benjamin Rush to Thomas Jefferson, Dec. 17, 1811 in *The Letters of Benjamin Rush,* ed. Herbert Butterfield (Princeton, 1951), 1111.

[57] Philadelphia *Aurora*, Oct. 19, 1811.

of pusillanimity." These sentiments "will animate Congress (as they animate the conduct of every American)." In an article entitled "A Message to Congress," the Pittsburgh *Commonwealth* stated, "our honor is pledged . . . and is too precious to be sullied" by efforts to preserve "peace at the cost of honor."[58] Richard Leech informed Roberts that "the preservation of our Republican institutions—of our country's peace and honor" depended on the actions of the Republicans in Congress.[59] Governor Snyder told the state legislature that "we have not only exhausted the cup of forbearance, but tasted that of humiliation . . . our only hope of having our wrongs redressed and our rights respected . . . is by an appeal to the last resort."[60]

With these admonitions from their constituents and state officials, Pennsylvania's delegation, consisting of seventeen Republicans and one Federalist, listened to the president's message. Presenting evidence of Britain's "hostile inflexibility in trampling our rights," Madison urged Congress to put the "United States into an armor and an attitude demanded by the crisis and corresponding with the national spirit and expectations."[61]

Whether this message was really stronger than his earlier communications and presaged the request for a declaration of war is a debatable point.[62] The people of Pennsylvania read it as a more militant message. On reading it Leech perceived "that strong measures are expected to be pursued and so far as I am able to see it is right . . . a continuance of a policy too amiable . . . may have a tendency to break and destroy that spirit of indignation so necessary to preserve the honor of the

---

[58] Oct. 14, 1811.
[59] Leech to Roberts, Nov. 8, 1811, Roberts Papers.
[60] *Pennsylvania Archives*, 4th series, IV, 763.
[61] *Annals of Congress*, 12th Cong., 1st sess., 11.
[62] Perkins, *Prologue to War*, 296-98.

nation. . . . Our policy therefore ought to be marked by a decision that cannot be mistaken."[63] Jones told Senator Gregg that "Congress must honor the request of the president and prepare the nation to protect its honor and assert its rights" by resort to war if necessary.[64] The Pittsburgh *Commonwealth* noted "a general coincidence of opinion on the subject of the president's message . . . the whole body of republicans have rallied round the administration and with one voice send forth their acclamation. . . . Let congress systematize the plans delineated by the president." When Britain learns that the United States is "preparing to exact that justice at the cannon's mouth which [has been] in vain solicited by sacrifices and concessions" it will either guarantee our rights or they will be "wrested from her on the field."[65] "Even at this late hour," a correspondent wrote to the Washington *Reporter,* the American government will "act with the firmness and decision which they appear so long to have been destitute of and retrieve that national character which . . . seems to have been almost extinguished."[66] Because the president intimated in his message that war was probable, a member of the Pennsylvania House introduced resolutions supporting the administration, and pledging the state to contribute willingly whatever should be asked of it by the nation.[67] Governor Snyder interpreted the message to mean that "a last appeal must be made to arms" to protect the rights, honor, and independence of the nation.[68]

[63] Leech to Roberts, Nov. 8, 1811, Roberts Papers.

[64] Jones to Gregg, Nov. 11, 1811, Jones Papers.

[65] Pittsburgh *Commonwealth,* Nov. 25, 1811.

[66] Washington *Reporter,* Dec. 27, 1811. See also Pennsylvania *Republican,* Dec. 24, 1815; Dauphin *Guardian,* Dec. 23, 1816.

[67] The resolutions are in *Pennsylvania House Journal,* 1811-1812, p. 42. The speech from which the quotation is taken is in Niles *Register,* Dec. 28, 1811, pp. 297-99.

[68] Speech by the governor quoted in Pittsburgh *Commonwealth,* Dec. 6, 1811.

In response to the message, the House Foreign Affairs Committee, of which John Smilie was a member, issued a report asserting that "we have borne with injury until forbearance has ceased to be a virtue."[69] Defending the report and the committee's recommendation for increases in the military establishment, committee chairman Porter stated that "all hopes of accommodating our differences with Great Britain by negotiation must be abandoned." Reciting a long list of grievances, he concluded that Britain's conduct toward us was not regulated by a sense of justice, "but solely by a regard to our probable forbearance." On the basis of this conclusion, the committee unanimously declared that "on the ground of mere pecuniary calculation, a calculation of profit and loss, it would be to our interest to go to war." But the subject presented itself to the committee from another point of view, "and that was as regarded the character of the country." Comparing our situation to that of a young man who, if he did not defend his honor when it was first attacked, "might safely calculate to be kicked and cuffed" the rest of his life, Porter concluded that "we should clearly understand and define those rights we ought to support, and should support them at every hazard."[70]

This speech was printed in its entirety in every Republican newspaper consulted, and the editors of two newspapers which were not consulted spoke favorably of it in their correspondence.[71] Editorially, the press emphasized the second part of the speech. Hopefully, the *Reporter* suggested, Congress's "concern for the nation's honor will be matched by an equal concern for its defences." The Pittsburgh *Commonwealth* hoped that "honorable sentiments will be followed by honorable action."

[69] *Annals of Congress*, 12th Cong., 1st sess., 373-77.
[70] *Annals of Congress*, 12th Cong., 1st sess., 415.
[71] Binns to Roberts, Nov. 14, 1811, Higgins to Roberts, Nov. 18, 1811, Roberts Papers.

Advocating a quick declaration of war to defend the nation's "rights and honor," the Pittsburgh *Mercury* headlined its editorial on the committee's report and Porter's speech "how soon?" These newspapers complimented Smilie for his role in the formulation of the report, and for his and Adam Seybert's speeches urging support of it.[72]

The Republican majority in Congress enacted the proposals of the Foreign Affairs Committee by immense majorities. Of the six resolutions the one with the least support carried by a vote of 110-22; that with the most support, 120-8. In both instances the Pennsylvania delegation, including the Federalist, James Milnor, voted unanimously to support the preparedness recommendations of the committee. On the four other resolutions, there were never more than three Pennsylvanians in opposition, though there were some who did not vote. On two proposals to amend the resolutions the Pennsylvania delegation voted 17-0-1 with the majority to defeat one, but split 9-8-1 on the proposal to allow merchant ships to arm in self defense.[73] Obviously, the Pennsylvania delegation had interpreted the president's message as a request for war preparations. Manuel Eyre felt "gratified . . . at such majorities in supporting the government in a manly attitude to defend and protect the rights and honor of our country; the stronger your measures and the more war-like your determination, the more probable that peace on honorable terms will result."[74] During the remainder of the session Pennsylvania Republicans approved of every strong measure taken by Congress on a variety of grounds, but considerations of national honor,

[72] Washington *Reporter*, Dec. 11, 1811; Pittsburgh *Commonwealth*, Dec. 2, Dec. 26, 1811; Pittsburgh *Mercury*, Dec. 3, Dec. 17, 1811.

[73] *Annals of Congress*, 12th Cong., 1st sess., 419-20, 545, 546, 547, 565.

[74] Eyre to Findley, Jan. 12, 1812, Gallatin Papers, New York Historical Society.

the national character, or the nation's independence always loomed large.

In the debate on the war tax measures, Seybert denied the right of congressmen to vote against a particular tax because it fell disproportionately on his constituents. The United States was about to engage in a war not to protect its commerce, but "to maintain our honor, liberty, and sovereignty as a nation," he told the House. The demands of the nation should take precedence over local inconveniences.[75] The *Reporter* grieved at the failure of the House to levy a tax on imported salt. It did not like the tax, but, given "Congress's determination to fight for our rights," it could not see how the House could refuse the ways and means. "The argument of unequal operation will apply to any tax," and therefore must defeat any measure. "When the honor and independence of the nation is at stake, legislators ought not to be moved by considerations of a local nature."[76] Thomas Rogers wrote Jonathan Roberts that he was dissatisfied with the slow pace in Congress: "We have suffered and suffered until forbearance has been pronounced cowardice and want of energy." The people, he felt, were ready for war, and he maintained that "their honor, as well as their property have been assailed." Congress must act "while national indignation remains high."[77]

In response to the public clamor and the president's request, Congress, on April 4, 1812, imposed an embargo on American shipping to last for ninety days. Republicans in Pennsylvania approved, seeing it as a precautionary measure, as the last step before a declaration of war.

[75] *Annals of Congress,* 12th Cong., 1st sess., 1116. The tax in question was on distilleries, and would have fallen heavily on Pennsylvania.

[76] Washington *Reporter,* March 9, 1812. For similar statements see Pittsburgh *Commonwealth,* March 17, Pittsburgh *Mercury,* March 19, Carlisle *Gazette,* March 11, Philadelphia *Aurora,* March 7, 1812.

[77] Rogers to Roberts, March 22, 1812, Roberts Papers.

Speaking in favor of the bill Adam Seybert asserted that
he felt pledged to go to war, and favored the embargo as a
maneuver to give shipping time to prepare and as a final
warning to the belligerents. Smilie favored the embargo
because "we must have war unless Great Britain relents,"
and he had always believed that "embargo must precede
war. . . . The embargo is intended as a war measure."[78]

Pennsylvanians approved of the embargo and the declaration of war which presumably would follow. The *Aurora*
called it a "harbinger of manly contest for essential rights
perseveringly trampled upon by the British government."
War will "cut deeply; but will be cheerfully and gloriously
borne in preference to a grovelling and dastardly submission to national dishonor." Duane urged Congress to make
adequate provision for enforcement because even at the
brink of war there were still those "who place personal
profit above the honor and independence of their country."[79]

The Pennsylvania *Republican* approved of the embargo
because Britain was vulnerable only by a cessation of
commercial intercourse. The Carlisle *Gazette* supported
the embargo on similar grounds. The embargo, it argued,
"is not war and does not inevitably lead to war. But it
must lead either to war, or to an honorable adjustment
with the belligerents." The measure "gives notice that
the period has arrived [in] which the manifold wrongs
we have received must be redressed." The *Gazette* concluded "it would be dishonorable if, without a redress
of our wrongs, war did not follow the expiration of the
embargo." No other alternative is left, "every other
expedient has been tried and failed."[80]

[78] *Annals of Congress*, 12th Cong., 1st sess., 1592.
[79] Philadelphia *Aurora*, April 2, April 4, April 6, April 7, 1812.
[80] Carlisle *Gazette*, April 7, 1812; Harrisburg *Republican*, April 7,
1812; Pittsburgh *Commonwealth*, April 8, April 15, 1812; Pittsburgh
Mercury, April 9, April 16, 1812; Washington *Reporter*, April 7, April 14,
1812.

In their strong concern for the nation's honor, Jonathan Roberts's correspondents expressed a similar approval of the embargo as a measure preparatory to war. Richard Leech wrote, "I have always been of the opinion that this nation could not be dragged into a war and that nothing but the maintenance of their rights and liberties could engage the people's consent." But he felt that at this time the "crisis has arrived and however great the calamities which may be apprehended . . . they will, I think, be incomparably less than those which would arise from submission to a base, deceitful and insulting foe." His brother Matthew, most of whose letters are nonpolitical, informed Roberts that "the circle I am acquainted with have pretty much made up their mind to . . . a war. Our condition cannot be worse than it has been and it is to the representatives of the nation we now look. . . . I think that that government which is found too weak for the protection of the property and honor of its citizens will be found to [*sic*] weak and unworthy of their support."

Rogers congratulated Roberts for his support of the embargo and urged quick legislation to make ready for battle. The American people "have done everything which human prudence could devise to avert war," he said, and were prepared to defend their honor. In a similar vein, Eyre told Roberts, "I feel with you the extent of the insults heaped upon us by Great Britain and would yield no more." He urged Roberts to call for war before the embargo expired, or the people would no longer believe in war.[81]

As the session of Congress continued the people became more impatient with the dalliance of their representatives. Few believed that Britain's policy would change or that any measure but war would be effective. Edward Fox

[81] Leech to Roberts, April 7, 1812, John Roberts to Roberts, April 12, 1812, Rogers to Roberts, April 20, 1812, Eyre to Roberts, April 19, May 2, 1812, Roberts Papers.

informed Roberts that there were two general grounds
for war: to obtain commerce "free and independent" and
"to establish a national character." On the basis of Britain's past actions we had ample grounds for war. If
Britain were allowed to continue its practices, it "in effect
recolonizes the United States. If then the objects of war
are to establish a national character, and if that can be,
even in reasonable probability, established by war the
suffering and expense of blood and treasure . . . should
. . . never once be brought into calculation."[82] A constituent who labeled himself a "simple farmer" told Roberts,
"it is the general wish and sentiment in the neighborhood
[Spread Eagle, Pennsylvania] that Congress will now go
on . . . in order to have their insulted country's rights
respected. We know that everything of a pacific nature
has been tried but without effect."[83] Major Isaac Anderson, who had served in the militia during the revolution
and viewed "with regret the war approaching the con-
fines of our horizon," could see no alternative. "What
could have been done by the United States . . . during a
painful, may I not say, shameful negotiation. . . . We have
been alternately cajoled and amused by promises falsely
made till the forbaring [sic] spirit of our country has
been exhausted and at last driven to the wretched alternative of war or a situation worse than colonial subjuga-
tion."[84] Another constituent expressed his wish "to live
at peace . . . but not to give up our rights as an independent nation."[85]

His regular correspondents described a growing feeling
for war in the state. At Roberts's request Rogers had
taken a "trip in the country" to ascertain the climate of
opinion. In his report he stated "the people are ready to

[82] Fox to Roberts, May 4, 1812 (two letters).
[83] Edward Stiles (?) to Roberts, May 30, 1812, Roberts Papers.
[84] Anderson to Roberts, May 13, 1812, Roberts Papers.
[85] William Slade to Roberts, May 11, 1812, Roberts Papers.

support any measure . . . to retrieve our lost honor. They anxiously wish and expect a declaration of war . . . . Never was there more unanimity among the people." The "honor and interest of our country demands [*sic*] an immediate declaration of war. The people looked for it."[86] John Binns told Roberts the people were convinced war was necessary to "pluck up our drowning honor." The longer Congress hesitated, "the feebler becomes the democratic party."[87] After the House had passed a declaration of war, Rogers expressed hope that the Senate would second their efforts and "save the Honor of our country." He told Roberts that if either of Pennsylvania's senators voted against the war "things will go badly with them."[88]

In a further effort to prepare for war, the president, pursuant to a law passed in April 1812, ordered 100,000 state militia detached to federal service. The governor's general orders of May 12, 1812, calling up the 14,000 requested from Pennsylvania, reflect the attitude of the state.

The revolution had scarcely been completed, said the governor, when the nation we had defeated began to invade our rights on the pretext of military necessity. The real reason was their "commercial jealousy and monopolizing animosity." The nation had endured these wrongs so long "that our motives have been mistaken and our national character misrepresented. Our forbearance had been called cowardice. Our love of peace a slavish fear of the dangers of war. . . . All means which wisdom and patriotism could devise have been in vain resorted to. The cup of patience—of humiliation and long suffering has been filled to overflowing." Reminding the people of the honor with which Pennsylvanians had fought in the revolution, he urged every citizen to act "as if the

86 Rogers to Roberts, May 16, May 24, 1812, Roberts Papers.
87 Binns to Roberts, May 3, 1812, Roberts Papers.
88 Rogers to Roberts, June 14, 1812, Roberts Papers.

public weal, the national honor, and independence, rested on his single arm."[89]

The response was gratifying to the governor. The 14,000-man quota was filled by volunteers. The letters offering the services of militia companies provide a further insight into the attitudes of the people. Many are straight-forward offers to serve, but many volunteers prefaced their offers with lengthy explanations.

Captain Henry Jarrett, commander of a volunteer company from Lower Nazareth township, stated that his troop decided to volunteer because "our country is insulted by foreign nations." The "accumulated insults heaped upon us by the British" must be avenged, and "the rights and liberties which were secured to us by the heroes of '76" must be regained.[90] The need to protect the rights for which the nation's forefathers fought and died, or to prove that Americans were not the "degenerate sons of gallant sires" are recurrent themes in these letters.[91] Some companies volunteered because it was their duty to defend the "only free government in the world" and the principles of republicanism.[92]

On the day Congress declared war John Grayson gave himself up "in mind and body to be a soldier in the service of my country's honor while the war lasted." Many must have done the same because "before many days plenty of volunteers had signed for filling the company and many were excluded."[93]

[89] *Pennsylvania Archives,* 2d series, XII, 531-33. There is a slightly different version of these orders in *Pennsylvania Archives,* 9th series, IV, 394-96.

[90] Jarrett to Snyder, June 2, 1812, *Pennsylvania Archives,* 2d series, XII, 541.

[91] Samuel Agnew to Snyder, May 14, 1812, *Pennsylvania Archives,* 2d series, XII, 553.

[92] Walter Lithgow to Snyder, undated, *Pennsylvania Archives,* 2d series, XII, 543. For other similar letters see ibid., 545-83.

[93] Autobiography of John Grayson, dated March 9, 1867. A typed copy of the manuscript is held by James O. Kehl at the University of Pittsburgh.

At a meeting in Washington, Pennsylvania, 1,200 Republicans resolved that "the only efficient remedy for the protracted and aggravated evils which afflict our country will be found in a prompt, vigorous, open war not for the limited and impoverished commerce of the moment, but for our inprescriptible rights of sovereignty. . . . These are the legitimate and inevitable causes of war."[94] In Carlisle a similar group resolved that "the cup of forbearance is full and the period has arrived when it becomes necessary to vindicate hour [sic] honor as a nation and regain that independence for which our fathers died."[95] Obviously, by the summer of 1812, Pennsylvania Republicans had become convinced that, in the words of Roger Brown, there was "no other option" but war or complete surrender.[96]

When Congress finally did declare war the action was justified on the grounds of national honor, and similar considerations were used to support continuation of the war after the orders-in-council, the express grievance for which war had been declared, had been repealed.

In a Fourth of July oration Richard Rush averred that after every effort to protect its rights by peaceful means the nation had "determined on appealing to the sword, not on the ground of immediate pressure alone, but on the still higher one that longer submission . . . holds out a prospect of permanent evil, a prospect rendered certain by the experience we have ourselves acquired, that forbearance . . . has not only invited a repetition, but an augmentation of trespasses increasing in bitterness as well as number." Any one of more than a dozen incidents could have been counted "an insult to our sovereignty and honor [each] in itself a cause for war."[97]

94 Washington *Reporter*, June 8, 1812.
95 Carlisle *Gazette*, June 12, 1812.
96 The phrase is the title of chapter two of his *Republic in Peril*.
97 Printed in the Philadelphia *Aurora*, July 24, July 25, 1812.

The editor of the Pittsburgh *Mercury* argued that Britain's intransigence and the failure of all our "pacific efforts" had left the nation but two alternatives. "We must either abandon the ocean or manfully assert and demand our rights. . . . Our government has chosen the latter. To have done otherwise would have been a cowardly surrender of the rights which God and Nature gave us."[98] Every Pittsburgh newspaper published the resolutions of over four thousand patriots who approved "of the manly and dignified ground which the government of the United States has assumed in manifesting its determination to maintain those rights by the sword, a just respect for which it has failed to preserve by nego-ciacion [*sic*]."[99]

To a publicly posed question, "Whether the war recently declared be necessary and expedient," Congressman Abner Lacock stated that the answer "will depend entirely on the worth and value we may attach to our present form of government and our national independence." Further "forbearance and submission to British insult and injury," he assured his listeners, "would have been an absolute surrender of national independence." Continued negotiation and forbearance "has been construed . . . into cowardice." "Nothing remained but resistance or submission. The former has been chosen as an evil infinitely less in itself than absolute surrender of national sovereignty."[100]

Denying the Federalist argument that "by repeal of the orders-in-council, the cause of war was extinct," Duane argued that there were many other causes for war not the least of which were "the many insults to honor," among which he named Britain's unwillingness to negotiate and failure to abide by her agreements. From here it was but

[98] July 9, July 16, 1812.

[99] Pittsburgh *Mercury*, Sept. 24, 1812; Pittsburgh *Commonwealth*, Sept. 25, 1812; Pittsburgh *Gazette*, Sept. 26, 1812.

[100] Pittsburgh *Mercury*, Aug. 13, Aug. 20, 1812.

a short step to the argument that "the prince's repeal is so well guarded by conditions and whereas's" that it was hardly a repeal at all. But, even accepting the repeal at its face value, there was no assurance if the declaration of war were repealed, that the orders would not be re-imposed.[101] The war must be continued to "prove that republicanism will prevail . . . that government based on the will of the people can protect their rights even against the most determined tyrant."[102] Jonathan Roberts had writ-ten to William Jones in the same vein. The war must be fought to a military conclusion "to prove republican gov-ernment capable of waging war."[103]

The Republican press viewed the presidential election in similar terms. The major question, as they saw it, was "whether the principles of the declaration of independence will be prostrated . . . or cherished and upheld by the people; whether a war for national sovereignty and inde-pendence—a war for our republican form of government . . . shall receive the countenance and support of the people."[104]

The *Aurora* took the overwhelming Republican victory in Pennsylvania elections as proof that the people ap-proved of the war and were determined to fight to main-tain "their rights, their freedoms and the independence of their nation." It was also proof that a government based "on the will of the people can rely on the honor of the people."[105]

As late as August 1813, Republicans argued along the

101 Philadelphia *Aurora*, Aug. 11, Aug. 13, Aug. 20, 1812.

102 Philadelphia *Aurora*, Sept. 3, 1812. The Pennsylvania *Republican* Aug. 25, 1812, expresses the same sentiments.

103 Roberts to Jones, Sept. 17, 1812, Jones Papers. Roberts had ex-pressed similar sentiments much earlier. See *Annals of Congress,* 12th Cong., 1st sess., 502-506.

104 Carlisle *Gazette,* Oct. 12, 1812. See also Philadelphia *Aurora,* Oct. 13, Pittsburgh *Commonwealth,* Oct. 9, Pittsburgh *Mercury,* Oct. 8, Wash-ington *Reporter,* Oct. 7, Pennsylvania *Republican,* Oct. 27, 1812.

105 Philadelphia *Aurora*, Oct. 21, 1812.

same lines. To the Federalist charge that war was declared because of Republican antipathy to Britain, the *Commonwealth* replied that "the republicans had a complete ascendency in the country . . . more than eleven years before war was declared." During that time every effort was made to avert war. When these efforts failed "no alternative remained but resistance by force of arms or submission to insufferable and endless injury and outrage."

The *Commonwealth* said that the Federalists knew that "Republicans were willing to make every sacrifice for peace except the honor and independence of their country." The Washington *Reporter* asserted in the same month that "this is a war primarily in defence of our rights and honor, liberty and independence."[106]

What emerges from this recitation of changing attitudes is not a finely articulated program proposed by any one group intent on war for a single purpose, but a broad judgment, informed by common sentiments, that preservation of the nation's independence and honor demanded war.

[106] Pittsburgh *Commonwealth,* Aug. 4, 1813; Washington *Reporter,* Aug. 30, 1813.

CHAPTER FOUR

Pennsylvania and
Economic Coercion

The military stalemate in the Anglo-French war prompted each nation to enact measures aimed at destroying the other's economy. The effect of the British orders-in-council and the French decrees was to make most American trade subject to confiscation by one or the other belligerent. The initial response of the American government was to protest the violations of American neutral rights and to appeal to both governments to modify their commercial legislation.[1]

Diplomatic efforts proved unavailing. When British violations of American rights increased substantially in the spring and summer of 1806, the American government was ready to consider more direct measures to persuade Britain to change its policy.[2] These measures took the form of economic legislation designed to deprive Great Britain of its American market and of American raw materials, on which, it was generally believed, Britain's economy depended. From the first retaliatory measure proposed in Congress to the outbreak of the war in June 1812, Pennsylvania Republicans supported the administration's efforts at economic coercion. The debate on the nonimportation bill of 1806 contains, in general, all the arguments which Pennsylvanians adduced in support of economic coercion during the next six years.

When he introduced a bill providing that there should be no imports from Great Britain until satisfactory arrangements were made between the United States and Britain, Representative Andrew Gregg, who as a senator in 1812 was only a moderate supporter of the war, defended the measure as an alternative to war. Britain's attacks on American rights were so great, he asserted, that they "may be considered as sufficient cause on which to ground a declaration of war." However, he was unwilling to resort to war "until other measures which we have in our power are tried."[3] John Smilie and Joseph Clay of Pennsylvania supported Gregg's resolutions on similar grounds in lengthy speeches during the subsequent debate.[4]

After two months of intermittent discussion, Gregg in an eloquent plea in support of his proposal maintained that one of the results of nonimportation would be to give an impetus to American manufacturing from which the entire nation would prosper. So long as the United States remained economically dependent on Great Britain, he argued, the former's political independence could not be complete.[5] He concluded the speech by conceding that he would be willing to yield his opinion if the House preferred "something more energetic" because he considered "unanimity . . . all important" to show their

---

[1] Irving Brant, *James Madison: Secretary of State* (Indianapolis, 1953), 160-76, 254-56.

[2] Bradford Perkins, *Prologue to War: England and the United States 1805-1812* (Berkeley, 1961), 69-72, 84-95, 177-80; Roger Brown, *Republic in Peril* (New York, 1964), 16-17.

[3] *Annals of Congress,* 9th Cong., 1st sess., 412.

[4] Ibid., 430-41.

[5] Ibid., 538-70.

enemies that "on all great national questions . . . we are
but one people."[6]

When, at the president's request, a more moderate nonimportation measure was introduced, Gregg indicated his
willingness to support it on the grounds that "a weak
measure carried by a great majority will be more powerful
than a strong measure carried by a small majority."[7] Pri-
vately he confided to William Jones that he would support any measure because a government that takes no
action in the face of repeated aggressions against its
rights "cannot long expect the support of the people."[8]
Smilie wrote in the same vein to Albert Gallatin. "If the
government does not do 'something,'" he warned, "it will
lose the confidence of the people."[9]

The action of the Pennsylvania delegation during the
debate on nonimportation reflects a similar concern on the
need for some action, and for party solidarity. On the
rollcall votes taken on Gregg's resolution, the Pennsylvania
delegation cast fifteen votes in its favor, with only one,
Michael Leib, voting consistently against. Joseph Clay
and James Kelly, when they voted, were not consistently
on either side. However, when it became known that
Jefferson preferred a less stringent substitute, the entire
delegation, including Gregg and Leib, switched to support it and voted unanimously for its passage—all but
Kelly, who did not vote.[10]

In the subsequent debates on the embargo, the nonintercourse bill and Macon's bill No. 2, the same themes, with
variations to fit the particular occasion, appeared again
and again. Economic coercion is a viable alternative to

6 Ibid., 549.
7 Ibid., 743.
8 Gregg to Jones, April 17, 1806, Jones Papers.
9 Smilie to Gallatin, March 9, 1806, Gallatin Papers.
10 *Annals of Congress*, 9th Cong., 1st sess., 767, 823, 877,

war and fosters the development of domestic manufacturing; administration measures must be supported by the
party lest lack of unity be interpreted as a sign of weakness; and measures to defend the nation's rights must be
passed unless voters look for other leadership.

As a coercive measure nonimportation proved a dismal
failure. Passed on April 18, 1806, its application was
delayed until December 14, 1807, and whatever effect it
might have had on the belligerents cannot be determined.[11] The Pennsylvania Republican press approved
of the measure as an effective weapon against Great
Britain and never failed to point out the impetus its enforcement would give to domestic manufactures. During
the summer and fall of 1806 several newspapers began
to show annoyance at the government's failure to enforce
the act. The Washington *Reporter* attributed the delay
to "Federalists and Merchants to whom profit means more
than honor." The Carlisle *Gazette* condemned those who
opposed enforcement and upbraided them as "short sighted
men who cannot see the great advantages which may
grow from temporary inconvenience."[12] The Federalist
press opposed nonimportation by relying on seemingly
contradictory arguments. It maintained that nonimportation was a weak measure which would never cause our
rights to be respected. On the other hand, it argued the
measure was so restrictive that it seriously damaged our
trade. The only positive suggestion made by the Federalists was that Congress keep the law on the books but
continue suspending its application thereby retaining a

[11] Herbert Heaton, "Non-Importation, 1806-1812," *Journal of Economic History,* I (November, 1941), 187-98.

[12] Washington *Reporter,* May 17, May 31, June 2, June 22, July 6,
July 27, Aug. 4, Aug. 25, 1806; Carlisle *Gazette,* May 20, May 27, June
3, June 24, July 1, July 8, July 22, Aug. 5, Aug. 26, 1806; see also
Pittsburgh *Gazette,* May 16, May 23, June 6, July 4, July 26, 1806;
Philadelphia *Aurora,* June 17, June 19, June 23, July 11, July 24, July 27,
Aug. 5, Aug. 9, Aug. 22, 1806.

club with which to threaten those who violated rights of the United States.[13]

Congress was soon deluged with memorials requesting repeal of the measure. One of these, from Philadelphia merchants, introduced by Joseph Clay, argued that the measure hurt their trade and served only to irritate Great Britain. Clay moved that the petition be referred to the Committee of Commerce and Manufactures and a long debate ensued. As with previous debates on similar petitions those who favored referral argued that the petition should be given respectful consideration because of the constitutional guarantee of the right of petition. Those who opposed argued that referral would imply that Congress was considering repeal of nonimportation, and retreating from the "high ground" it had taken by passing the measure. John Smilie stated that the extensive debate on the Philadelphia memorial gave it more significance than it deserved, or that Clay had intended when he introduced it. He concluded by asserting that the memorial had been drawn up by "a party in favor of the British government to embarrass the operations of our government." The motion to refer the petition lost 50-70, the Pennsylvania delegation siding with the majority by a 7-11 division.[14]

The failure of nonimportation to effect a change in British policy, and Britain's continued violations of America's maritime rights prompted many to demand, and the president to request, a more effective measure. To a Congress called to meet earlier than usual, Jefferson submitted his proposal for an embargo on December 18, 1807. The president's message was referred to a committee of which Senator Gregg of Pennsylvania was a member. On the

13 Pittsburgh *Gazette*, June 7, June 21, June 28, Aug. 4, Aug. 18, 1806; Pennsylvania *Gazette*, May 5, May 12, May 19, June 2, June 16, July 14, July 28, 1806.
14 *Annals of Congress*, 10th Cong., 1st sess., 961-82.

same day the committee reported a bill "laying an embargo on all ships and vessels in the ports and harbors of the United States." After approving a motion by a vote of 22-7 to suspend the rules requiring that a bill introduced into the Senate must be read three times on three separate days and defeating by a vote of 12-16 a motion to postpone consideration of the measure for one day, the Senate passed the embargo by a vote of 22-6. On every vote Gregg sided with the majority while Samuel Maclay, Pennsylvania's other senator, voted with the minority.[15]

On December 22 the House, in secret session, began consideration of the Senate embargo bill. Neither the *Annals of Congress* nor the *Journal of the House of Representatives* report any extended debate on the bill, but five rollcall votes were taken before the bill was finally passed. Of these, three were taken to defeat limiting amendments and two to defeat opposition delaying tactics. Of seventeen Pennsylvania congressmen attending on that day, eleven voted with the majority to defeat every amendment or delaying tactic, while only one, William Hoge, voted on every issue with the Federalist minority. On the final vote to pass the embargo as it was submitted, the Pennsylvania delegation split 12-5-1 in favor of passage. The Pennsylvania delegation provided more votes for passage of the embargo than any other delegation.[16]

On December 27, 1807, the House began consideration of legislation to enforce the embargo. Debate on the enforcement legislation took more than a week with numerous amendments, procedural votes, and attempts at delay introduced by the opposition. Only two members of the Pennsylvania delegation took part in the debate. Speaking against an amendment to exempt ships involved in the fisheries, William Milnor observed that although he had

---

[15] *Annals of Congress,* 10th Cong., 1st sess., 50-51.
[16] *Annals of Congress,* 10th Cong., 1st sess., 1217-22.

voted against the embargo, since it had been passed, he wished it to be "carried into full effect—that there should be no evasion." Furthermore, he argued, this amendment would expose the men of the fisheries fleet to impressment thereby defeating another purpose of the embargo—keeping our ships in port in order to avoid incidents that might lead to war. Smilie took the floor after Milnor. He pointed out that everyone suffered to some degree because of the embargo, but that the measure was necessary to protect "our valuable national rights." Its effectiveness as an alternative to war would be blunted if any exceptions were made. If exceptions were made for the fishermen today, there would be justification for making other exemptions tomorrow and the embargo would fail completely.

During the debate numerous rollcall votes were taken and the Pennsylvania delegation voted much as it had during the embargo debate. Twelve members always voted with the majority against any exemptions, against any amendment weakening the enforcement measure and against any delaying tactic. Only one, William Hoge, always voted with the minority in support of such measures. The remaining five, though generally siding with the minority, cast some votes, on some issues, with the majority. On January 2, 1808, the enforcement bill passed the House, 73-22. With the exception of Hoge and Samuel Smith who did not vote, the entire Pennsylvania delegation voted in favor of this measure.[17]

Throughout the remainder of the session the House considered numerous amendments to the embargo and the enforcement legislation and many memorials and petitions from various parts of the country desiring relief or exemption from the embargo laws. Congress, with the support of the Pennsylvania delegation, remained stead-

[17] *Annals of Congress,* 10th Cong., 1st sess., 1244-55, 1269-71.

fast. Weakening amendments were invariably defeated, and no exemptions were granted. In the Pennsylvania delegation the division remained the same. Twelve members voted always with the majority, Hoge always with the minority, while five members shifted from one side to the other.[18]

One incident is particularly revealing. On January 4, 1808, Mr. John Porter of Pennsylvania introduced a memorial from Philadelphia merchants praying that ships that had been loaded and had secured clearance papers before the passage of the act be "excepted from the general embargo." Milnor and Smilie spoke in favor of Porter's motion to refer the memorial to the Committee of Commerce and Manufactures. On the question of referral the House decided 91-16 to refer the memorial, the Pennsylvania delegation voting unanimously in favor. One week later the committee, of which Porter was a member, reported unanimously against granting the merchants' petition on the now familiar grounds that any exemptions would blunt the effectiveness of the embargo as an alternative to war and might result in incidents leading to hostilities. By forcing the nation to rely on its own resources, the embargo would also hasten American development and secure the economic basis necessary to make political independence a reality. The committee's report was referred to a committee of the whole where its recommendations were approved by a substantial majority. The Pennsylvania delegation divided 14-4. The twelve who always voted with the majority were joined by James Kelly and Joseph Clay. Hoge was joined by Robert Jenkins, William Milnor, and Samuel Smith.[19]

[18] For rollcall votes on measures dealing with enforcement of the embargo, or petitions praying exemptions see *Annals of Congress,* 10th Cong., 1st sess., 1269, 1271, 1276, 1384, 2245, 2260, 2261, 2262, 2263.

[19] *Annals of Congress,* 10th Cong., 1st sess., 1271-77, 1383-87; *Journal of the House of Representatives,* 10th Cong., 1st sess., 270-71.

Speaking in support of an addition to the enforcement legislation, Joseph Clay stated that he had not favored the embargo and had not voted for it (he was the absent member). However, he believed it to be everyone's duty to make the law effective once Congress committed itself to the principle of the embargo and he would therefore vote in favor of the enforcement measure. Smilie contended that those who opposed the enforcement legislation were those who had opposed the embargo and hoped, by their opposition to this legislation, to make it ineffective. Had they forgotten, he asked the members, the precarious situation of the nation at the time of the original legislation? At that time, he contended, the nation had but three choices, "either submit to all injuries, . . . go to war, or lay an embargo." Congress had chosen the last as the most desirable alternative calculated to secure the rights of the United States without resort to war. Those who opposed the embargo and the enforcement legislation offered only war or submission, neither of which alternatives he was willing to accept.[20]

The last important measure relative to the embargo undertaken during this session was a bill authorizing the president to suspend the embargo during the congressional recess if, in his opinion, conditions warranted such action. The debate began on April 8, 1808, when Congressman George Washington Campbell of Tennessee introduced such a resolution in the House. It was referred to the committee of the whole without a division where, on the next day, debate began in earnest. The debate continued until April 19 with many members taking part in the discussion, but not one delegate from Pennsylvania participated. Part of the opposition, led by John Randolph, argued that the bill unconstitutionally delegated power to the president. A smaller group, headed by D. R. Wil-

[20] *Annals of Congress*, 10th Cong., 1st sess., 1706, 1710.

liams, opposed the bill on the grounds that its passage
might be interpreted by foreign powers as a sign of
weakness.

The proponents of the bill argued along two lines. One
argument maintained that granting the president the
power to suspend the embargo would impress upon the
people that the measure had been forced on the administration by Great Britain, not arbitrarily imposed by the
government, and that only a change in British policy
would justify removal of the embargo. The other argument maintained that since the embargo was a retaliatory
measure to coerce the belligerents to alter their policy
without war, the act should be suspended if the desired
changes were effected.

During the debate many amendments were introduced
but all were defeated by sizable majorities. Only three
votes are recorded, however. The Pennsylvania delegation followed its established pattern. Those who habitually
sided with the majority did so on each of the three amendments, while Hoge and the waverers voted with the
minority. The bill finally passed the House 60-36, with
Pennsylvania dividing 12-2-4. The four not voting were
all of the group without definite commitment.[21]

Thus, a review of the embargo debate shows quite
clearly that a majority of the Pennsylvania congressmen
accepted economic coercion as an alternative to war, and
looked to the possibility of the benefits to be derived
from the impetus it would give to domestic manufacturing.
The votes of the Pennsylvania delegation reflect the concern for party unity. The twelve representatives who
always voted with the majority were all Republicans.
Hoge, who was always with the minority, and James Kelly
of Adams County were the only Federalists on the dele-

[21] *Annals of Congress*, 10th Cong., 1st sess., 2066, 2083-2171, 2198-
2246.

gation. The party affiliation of the other four who vacil-
lated from one side to the other cannot be definitely
determined. Samuel Smith was elected with Federalist
support in Pittsburgh, but he ran on a coalition ticket of
Federalists and disaffected Republicans. William Milnor
of Philadelphia was the candidate of a Republican faction
in the city and probably drew some Federalist support
since the Federalists did not run a candidate in that
election. Robert Jenkins was an "irregular" Republican
"inclined to wander from the party line." He, Daniel
Hiester, and Matthias Richards had been elected on a
ticket sponsored jointly by Federalists and Constitutional
Republicans from a district consisting of Chester, Lancaster, and Berks counties. William Findley, writing to
former Congressman Joseph Hiester, referred to Samuel
Smith and William Hoge as members "of a flying squad
who called themselves republicans but on whom we could
not depend unless that we knew several of them would
almost always vote against us."[22]

The same themes can be found in the Republican press
of the state and in the correspondence of leading Pennsylvania Republicans. The Carlisle *Gazette* called the
embargo a "judicious measure." It protected American
property, preserved peace and neutrality, and would gain
respect for American rights from those nations who
violated them. It urged the people to rally to the government and support the embargo in order to prove to the
world "that republican government can protect the people
and attain its ends by methods short of war."[23] A correspondent declared the embargo was fully justified although it would create hardship. But he felt most of the

[22] Sanford Higginbotham, *Keystone of the Democratic Arch: Pennsylvania Politics, 1800-1816* (Harrisburg, 1952), 73, 119, 157, 173, 372;
Paulson's American Daily Advertiser, Oct. 22, 1808; Findley to Hiester,
April 9, 1808, Gregg Collection.
[23] Carlisle *Gazette*, Jan. 8, 1808.

inconveniences would have been inevitable since "all the belligerent nations being placed in a state of blockade . . . would have produced the same result; there is this difference in favor of the embargo. By it we preserve our seamen and property and we vitally affect the nations which have injured us."[24] Both the Washington *Reporter* and the Pittsburgh *Commonwealth* argued that the embargo would force a change in British policy and "cause our rights to be respected." Both papers urged everyone to support the law and the administration in order to prove that there are methods of coercion short of war. If the embargo did not succeed, more vigorous measures could be taken later.[25] In Harrisburg, the editor of the *Guardian* referred to the embargo as a "strong measure," the only weapon "competent to procure us justice." The Cumberland *Register* called it "a necessary and proper measure. . . . Its utility is beyond doubt."

The Philadelphia Republican press also supported the embargo in spite of the fact that its operation could be expected to injure the city's commercial interests. Duane had recommended an embargo as early as 1805. It would be an easy way to prostrate Great Britain and force her to respect American rights while it would avoid the threats to republican government inherent in the large military establishment and heavy burden of debt which a war, or preparations for war, would entail. "A suspension of intercourse," he argued, "would convert the whole West Indian interest in England, which is stronger than any other, into active enemies of the present ministry." He felt the embargo would incite insurrections throughout Great Britain if it were continued, and that it would force that nation

[24] Carlisle *Gazette*, Jan. 29, 1808.
[25] Washington *Reporter*, Dec. 19, Dec. 26, 1807, Jan. 2, Jan. 17, 1808; Pittsburgh *Commonwealth*, Feb. 12, Feb. 26, March 2, March 16, 1808; Dauphin *Guardian*, Jan. 5, April 11, 1808; Cumberland *Register*, Jan. 26, 1808.

to alter its policy toward America. The consequences of the embargo for the United States would be *"incalculably beneficial."* He said that some inconvenience may arise from want of a market for America's produce, but that this would be momentary because America's own industry would expand rapidly to create a new market. If this policy leads to war, Duane asserted, war must be accepted. "We have a long list of grievances . . . and must gain acknowledgment of our just and honest claims."[26] In July 1808, Duane reprinted a box from the Northampton *Republican Spy* which subsequently appeared in many Republican papers in the state.

THE EMBARGO

will produce temporary inconvenience; the loss of a few thousand dollars; and give a little more time to citizens who do not choose to turn their attentions to internal improvements. It will not starve anybody. On the contrary, the staple necessaries of life will be cheaper.

A WAR

will produce the loss of millions of dollars, burning and sacking of towns and cities, rape, theft, murders, streams of blood, weeping widows, hapless orphans, the beggary of thousands, the ruin of agriculture and an extensive depravation of morals.

Citizens of the United States! Which do you choose?[27]

John Binns shared these sentiments and praised the policy in his paper, the *Democratic Press.* He wrote to Roberts that the measure had everything to recommend it because after years of futile protest and abortive threats, "it is a mode of action. It manifests to Britain the importance

[26] Philadelphia *Aurora,* July 3, 1807. Philadelphia *Aurora,* Dec. 14, 1805, May 26, July 3, 1807.
[27] Philadelphia *Aurora,* July 26, 1808.

of American benevolence. It asserts our rights and pre-
serves the peace."[28]

After an initial burst of support, the Federalist press
opposed the embargo, but even the opposition accepted
the categories of the measure's proponents, and was never
as partisan, violent or obstructionist as the opposition of
New England Federalists. William Short wrote to Jefferson that Federalists in Philadelphia "are not in sentiment
with the insurgents of the North."[29] In Philadelphia,
Federalists supported temperate resolutions, "asserting
loyal support to the union 'whatever may be the errours
of the administration, and however severe the pressure
which these errours may have occasioned.' "[30] Federalist
editors simply argued that the embargo was not an honorable alternative to war, and would not cause Britain to
respect American rights. Even if it were to succeed, the
cost would be too high. Before the embargo could have
any effect on the nation's enemies, at least a year must
elapse, wrote the editor of the Pittsburgh *Gazette*. In the
meantime "the merchant must lay his ships up in his
docks . . . the planter and farmer destroy their super-
fluous produce. All will become bankrupt to no avail."
England would be deprived of some necessities, but this
would not cause a change in policy nor deter the fight
against Napoleon.[31] The Harrisburg *Times* warned that
the embargo would "stagnate all trade and embarrass
every portion of the citizens in the community." Its
passage was an "admission of American weakness; that
we cannot protect our trade and therefore are willingly

[28] Higginbotham, *Keystone*, 166; Binns to Roberts, Jan. 11, 1808,
Roberts Papers.
[29] Short to Jefferson, Sept. 6, 1808, *The Writings of Thomas Jefferson*,
ed. A. A. Lipscomb and A. E. Bergh (Washington, D.C., 1903), XII, 159.
[30] Cited in Higginbotham, *Keystone*, 239-40.
[31] Pittsburgh *Gazette*, Jan. 12, 1808; *Paulson's American Daily Advertiser*, Dec. 24, 1807; J. Cutler Andrews, *Pittsburgh's Post-Gazette* (Boston, 1936), 47.

giving it up." The Pennsylvania *Gazette* commented that "the policy of commercial restriction will ruin this country before it effects a change of policy" in France or England. It is not a "vigorous measure," but another attempt to give "inaction the color of activity."[32] The virulence with which Federalists attacked the embargo must have been more a matter of political opposition to the Jefferson administration than of actual discomfort induced by economic privation.

Republicans did not allow Federalist allegations to go unchallenged, especially after they received the news of the resolutions of the Massachusetts legislature urging defiance of, and noncompliance with, the embargo and the enforcement legislation. The Carlisle *Gazette* urged compliance with the embargo act which the United States had been "compelled to resort to in vindication of its rights and to induce the British government to refrain from the plunder and oppression of our citizens and property." Those who opposed the measure and urged noncompliance, argued the editor, were moved by narrow and personal interests, and refused to see the benefits the nation could derive from the act. If the act was obeyed, either England would be forced to change its policy, or the United States, compelled to rely upon itself for necessities, would develop its industry more quickly. "By producing from our own resources what we should otherwise have carried our money abroad to obtain, we keep our money in circulation at home." This would lead to an increase in manufacturing which, in turn, would create an "industrial class" creating a new market for the farmer. Development of manufactures would force us to develop other resources and improve our transportation. This economic development would provide "new securi-

[32] Pennsylvania *Gazette*, March 11, April 17, 1808; Harrisburg *Times*, Dec. 28, 1807, Feb. 29, 1808.

ties for our independence" and new "value and strength to our freedom." Most importantly, "foreign influence, the bane of free states, diminishes in proportion as the national confidence in its own resources becomes better known and more duly appreciated."[33]

The *Aurora* also saw positive benefits to be derived. The happiness and security of the United States, wrote Duane, depended as much on the balance of its economy as on the republican balance of its government and its military strength. So long as the United States relied on foreign nations for any essential needs, the country could not be truly independent. It was, therefore, "gratifying to witness the good consequences which flow to our country from evil causes. The aggressions of Great Britain [which forced us to enact the embargo for] protection and retaliation will do more for us in twelve months than our own slow policy would have accomplished in 20 years." By forcing Americans to rely on themselves, Britain was underwriting the nation's independence.[34]

To counteract the Federalist argument that the embargo would not affect Britain's economy, Duane published long extracts from British newspapers and the parliamentary debates to show that it was having the desired effect. He gave particular prominence to the memorials of British merchants petitioning Parliament to adjust its differences with the United States so trade would be reopened. He published the complete text of Alexander Baring's *An Enquiry into the Causes and Consequences of the Orders in Council of Great Britain Towards the Neutral Commerce of America*. After the last installment he stated that if the British government sought more information from men like Baring instead of relying on the misinformation it received from Federalists, the differ-

[33] Carlisle *Gazette*, Nov. 28, 1808.
[34] Philadelphia *Aurora*, July 2, 1808.

ence between the two countries could easily be adjusted to the satisfaction of both nations.[35]

Similar sentiments were expressed in the western part of the state. On March 6, 1809, the Washington *Reporter* condemned "mercantile characters . . . who depend for life and fortune on British goods." The embargo had helped the development of new industries as witnessed "by the many new establishments in this county." But the *Reporter* warned that England would use any means "*to crush the American mechanic and manufacturer by underselling them.*" Those who were interested in the prosperity of their country rather than their own personal wealth would support all administration measures to keep the peace, defend the nation's rights, and foster economic development.[36]

The Pittsburgh *Commonwealth,* pointing to increase in domestic manufactures and the prosperity and growth of the city, praised the embargo for the impetus it gave to economic growth and condemned those who opposed such a beneficial measure because of "personal inconvenience, party feeling or foreign attachment."[37]

Support of the embargo and condemnation of Federalist opposition was not limited to the press. A public meeting of Republicans in Washington County passed resolutions condemning the "hireling writers of a desperate British faction who . . . advocate treason." The meeting denounced Hoge for his votes in the House and blamed "the avarice of unprincipled speculators" for the failure of the embargo to force a change in British policy. The final resolution affirmed that because of the embargo "impor-

35 The publication of Baring's pamphlet begins on April 21, 1808, and continues, with interruptions, until the end of the month. Similar material appears regularly in the columns of the Philadelphia *Aurora,* but is particularly heavy in April and May, 1808.

36 Washington *Reporter,* March 6, 1809.

37 Pittsburgh *Commonwealth,* Feb. 19, 1809.

tant progress in the establishment of domestic manufactories" has been made. In the same meeting a letter
was sent to President Jefferson thanking him for his efforts
to preserve the honor, peace, and independence of the
country against foreign foes and "the worthless part of
the community" who put their personal gain above the
public welfare. The letter closed with a firm pledge to
support the government if it became necessary to use
force either to enforce the law or to secure the nation's
rights.[38]

In Philadelphia ten thousand people attended a meeting
to support the national government and to condemn the
Massachusetts legislature for its advocacy of treason.
In his opening address William Jones referred to the
embargo as a temporary measure which "must be superseded, either by the peaceful enjoyments of our commercial rights and independence, or their maintenance
at the point of the sword." The state attorney general
then offered the resolutions adopted by the meeting. These
denounced New England opposition to the embargo,
endorsed the measure as an honorable alternative to war,
and recognized the protection it gave to domestic manufactures. The final resolutions declared that if the embargo
had been rigidly enforced "it would have . . . prevented
the necessity of a recurrence to any other means to ensure
justice from the belligerent nations" and clarified the
meaning of "other means" by approving preparations for
war and pledging to support the government in any
"action" it should take, should Britain continue to violate
neutral rights.[39] At a second meeting, a week later, eighteen thousand persons declared their support of the resolutions adopted by the earlier meeting and again pledged

[38] Washington *Reporter,* Feb. 27, 1809.
[39] Philadelphia *Aurora,* Jan. 25, 1809.

to support the administration's efforts to protect American rights.[40]

In Pittsburgh a public meeting heartily endorsed the embargo and promised to support a war if the embargo did not win respect for American rights. In Harrisburg another meeting approved the embargo and promised to support any measure, including war, which might be adopted to uphold American rights.[41] Meetings which adopted similar resolutions took place in Erie, Lancaster, and Wilkes-Barre, Pennsylvania. The resolutions adopted at these public meetings state explicitly what the editorials and the press had already implied: that the embargo was an alternative to war and if it failed to be effective, war must be declared.

Public officials reflected the same attitude. A significant debate over the adoption of an address to the president developed in the legislative session of 1807-1808. This address expressed support for the policies of the national government, and approved its conduct of foreign affairs in general and the embargo in particular. The address also condemned the conduct of Great Britain and pledged the legislature to support every administration effort to protect American rights. It closed with a tribute to Jefferson's wisdom and patriotism which successfully "defended our rights and . . . saved the nation from the scourge of war." Every Federalist effort to substitute resolutions that did not mention the embargo or condemn the conduct of France was easily defeated.[42]

In the *American State Papers* there is a resolution sub-

[40] Philadelphia *Aurora*, Feb. 1, 1809.
[41] Pittsburgh *Commonwealth*, Feb. 22, 1809; Carlisle *Gazette*, March 3, 1809, copied the report of the Harrisburg meeting from the Dauphin *Guardian*, Feb. 28, 1809.
[42] *Pennsylvania House Journal*, 1807-1808, pp. 49-57, 86-91, 187-88; *Pennsylvania Senate Journal*, 1807-1808, pp. 5-11, 81-91.

mitted to Congress by the Pennsylvania legislature dated December 23, 1808, approving of the embargo as "a measure . . . calculated to induce an observance of our national rights without a resort to the horrors and desolations of war." If that pacific measure did not produce the desired effect the resolution promised to support whatever measures the government may take to preserve the nation's rights.[43] In his opening message to the state legislature in 1808, Governor McKean congratulated the people of Pennsylvania for the loyalty with which they had supported the federal government. The good-natured manner in which the state had suffered the inconveniences of the embargo, and the loyal pledges it had made to suffer even the inconvenience of war were proof of the willingness of the citizens of the state to pledge, once again, their "Lives, Liberties and . . . sacred honor to support the Declaration 'that these states are, and of Right ought to be free and independent.'" William Shippen confirms the impression of popular support for the embargo. In spite of it, he wrote to a friend in Boston, "the people again seem to be attaching themselves to the Democratic Party."[44]

The General Assembly, in its session of 1808-1809, passed a number of resolutions approving the policy of the national administration and pledging support of any future action it might take. The first set of resolutions was introduced by Jacob Mitchell, of Philadelphia. Because the critical situation of the government's relation to foreign powers "calls for all its energies, unanimity and patriotism," and because "in such times it is the duty of the constituted authorities to aid the common cause of the country," the General Assembly resolved that the embargo was a "just and necessary effect of the French de-

[43] *American State Papers: Foreign Affairs*, III, 294-95.
[44] *Pennsylvania Archives*, 4th series, IV, 650-51; William Shippen to Charles Bishop, Oct. 6, 1809, Shippen Papers, Library of Congress.

crees and British orders—as a measure of sound policy it meets with our decided approbation and as a means of preserving peace it is entitled to the support of all Americans." The assembly then pledged to support "with united hearts and hands . . . whatever measures may be resorted to in defense of our national rights . . . if the insolence, injustice, violence, or depravity of any power compell us to war, we will war with all our hearts and all our strength." These resolutions were debated and sent to a committee which, a week later, reported them with minor verbal changes and one significant addition. "The ocean being the equal property of all nations we will never abandon or surrender its rights . . . and our present *temporary* embargo shall never be considered . . . as an abandonment of our maritime rights." During the debate Federalists submitted substitute resolutions condemning the embargo "as an ineffective method of coercion in foreign affairs" and denouncing it as an abandonment of American rights "to free navigation of the seas." These Federalist resolutions were defeated by the same margin by which the Republican sponsored resolutions were passed: 72-20 in the House, 20-5 in the Senate. It is impossible to discover the party affiliation of all the members of the General Assembly. Of those whose party affiliation is known, however, the vote was strictly on party lines. It should be noted, also, that not one of the representatives from the city or county of Philadelphia, on which the embargo would weigh most heavily, ever voted with the minority.[45]

When the legislature received official news of the Massachusetts resistance to the embargo it considered an even

[45] The resolutions, votes, and a brief description of this debate are in *Pennsylvania House Journal*, 19th sess., 1808-1809, pp. 15-16, 35-38, 57, 71-75; *Pennsylvania Senate Journal*, 19th sess., 1808-1809, pp. 82, 17-90, 132-33. See also Higginbotham, *Keystone*, 183.

stronger set of resolutions denouncing as "enemies and traitors" any who sought to dissolve the Union. The House offered to furnish the federal government Pennsylvania militia if they should be needed to enforce the federal law in Massachusetts. These resolutions proceeded to a second reading on March 1, 1809, but no further action was taken probably because on that day Congress repealed the embargo.[46]

Like the resolutions passed by the public meetings, the resolutions and debates in the state legislature indicate that Pennsylvania supported the embargo as an alternative to war, but viewed it as a temporary measure which, if unsuccessful, must be followed by hostilities.

These public attitudes are also reflected in private correspondence. Jesse Higgins, a Republican newspaper editor, and Benjamin Rush, doctor, scholar, and leading citizen of Philadelphia, were men of different backgrounds and positions who mentioned the embargo often enough in their correspondence so that it is easy to trace the development of their attitudes. Writing to Jonathan Roberts about Federalist opposition, Higgins maintained that the Federalists were simple obstructionists who made no positive proposals. "[The Federalists] know as well as we do that one of two evils presented itself to the acceptance of the American government, an embargo, or war; and they know as well that the least evil was chosen."[47] In April he told Roberts that Baring's pamphlet proved the embargo "was much more effectual than a declaration of war." He said he "would not be surprised at hearing a recall of the British orders-in-council in very little time."[48]

[46] *Pennsylvania House Journal,* 19th sess., 1808-1809, pp. 530-32, 551-52, 583; *Pennsylvania Senate Journal,* 19th sess., 1808-1809, pp. 236-39, 292-97.
[47] Higgins to Roberts, Jan. 19, 1808, Roberts Papers.
[48] Higgins to Roberts, April 27, 1808, Roberts Papers.

As the months passed and Britain's policy did not change, Higgins's letters reflect his growing frustration. He continued to insist that the embargo would change British policy. "No possible benefit can accrue to England from . . . her orders-in-council." The continuance of the embargo subjected this nation "to all the evils which destruction of commerce can produce and the most unhappy attacks on our government from an unprincipled faction which seen [*sic*] to sacrifice . . . everything in order to [gain] a recovery of power and to obtain revenge of the Governing party." The expansion of domestic manufacturing and the steadfast support of all Republicans compensated in part for the destruction of commerce and the rejuvenation of the Federalists, but, Higgins warned, unless the orders-in-council were repealed quickly a new policy would be required. Subsequent letters indicate what the new policy would have to be because, he said, a "continuation of our pacific measures" would lead to Federalist gains. "Federal depravity and strength has attained a height I had not foreseen." Republican government "can never be safe so long as there is a party so depraved as to place its interests above national honor."[49]

Benjamin Rush feared particularly the increase in Federalist strength which he attributed to the embargo. "Great clamors are everywhere excited against the embargo," he wrote to John Adams. "How different were the feelings and conduct of our citizens in 1774. . . . The clamors originate . . . chiefly among one class of citizens."[50] Later he expressed his belief that large numbers of Republicans and all Federalists would support Clinton and Monroe, rather than Madison in the forthcoming presi-

[49] Higgins to Roberts, June 28, July 3, July 5, July 22, Aug. 14, Aug. 23, Aug. 30, Sept. 15, 1808, Roberts Papers.

[50] Benjamin Rush to John Adams, Feb. 18, 1808, in Herbert Butterfield, *Letters of Benjamin Rush*, 2 vols. (Princeton, 1951), II, 960.

dential election and the Federalist candidate for governor in the state elections.[51] Andrew Gregg informed William Jones that when he had voted for the embargo he believed that "it was a powerful engine in our hands which . . . could not fail of producing the intended effect." Violations which made the embargo ineffective and British intransigence, however, had "blunted its effect [and] weakened the confidence of the people in their government and in the administration." Britain, he was sure, had concluded that "we did not have the power to enforce our own laws, let alone conduct a war." He suggested that the government take measures to prove one or the other.[52]

It seems clear that a majority of Pennsylvania Republicans supported the embargo as an alternative to war, which would be supplanted by war if it did not achieve its intended goals. This was the policy urged by the Republican press and by the state legislature, and this was the mood of the Pennsylvania delegation when the second session of the Tenth Congress began on November 7, 1808. Beginning in mid-October 1808, and continuing well into February 1809, Republican newspapers carried articles and editorials demonstrating the effectiveness of the embargo. These also urged Congress not to submit to the pressure of foreign governments or domestic factions which, under a variety of disguises, urged a policy of submission. Concurrently there were numerous articles urging increases in the military establishment and other preparations for war. The tone of the Republican press was quite clear. Congress must either extend the embargo and enact effective enforcement legislation, or abandon efforts at peaceable coercion and declare war.

The state legislature approved resolutions to be sent

[51] Rush to Adams, July 13, Aug. 24, Sept. 22, 1808, ibid., 970, 976, 983, 984.
[52] Gregg to Jones, April 10, 1810, Jones Papers.

to Congress, and thanked the members of both houses "who have adhered to the wise and dignified policy of the executive in voting against repeal of the embargo laws." The resolutions concluded by proclaiming that "a repeal of the embargo laws at this time would in our opinion be an abandonment of the rights of the nation and of the property of citizens of the United States."[53]

On the third day of the session the Pennsylvania delegation voted unanimously to consider a motion calling for repeal of the embargo and all enforcement legislation. From the subsequent debate it is clear that Federalists supported the resolution with the hope of embarrassing the administration and repealing the embargo, while Republicans hoped to defeat repeal or substitute something stronger.[54] Having voted to consider the resolution, Smilie urged postponement of such consideration on the grounds that to consider the motion at that time, unless a substitute for the embargo were proposed would imply a willingness to surrender the independence of the country.[55]

For the next two months the Republicans defeated a barrage of Federalist attacks on the embargo, but they made no positive proposals of their own. Finally, on December 27, 1808, the House began consideration of a stringent enforcement measure. Debate on this bill was heated and lengthy with innumerable amendments, attempts at delay, and procedural arguments. No member of the Pennsylvania delegation took an active part in the debate, but their votes show that they continued to adhere to the Republican majority and to their previous positions. The division in the delegation varied between 15-2 and 13-4 (one member was absent), Robert Jenkins having joined Hoge in constant opposition. Kelly and Milnor

[53] *Pennsylvania House Journal*, 19th sess., 1808-1809, pp. 32, 53.
[54] *Annals of Congress*, 10th Cong., 2d sess., 474-78.
[55] *Annals of Congress*, 10th Cong., 2d sess., 475.

continued to shift from side to side. On the final vote passing the enforcement bill the Pennsylvania delegation divided 14-2 with Hoge not voting.[56] This measure proved to be the swansong of the united Republican majority. Defections among New England members and lack of executive leadership either from the lameduck Jefferson or the president-elect Madison caused a fragmentation of the party in Congress. Some Republicans continued to recommend strong measures to the extent of proposing a definite date for repeal of the embargo and the commencement of hostilities. Other Republicans introduced weak measures going so far as to recommend unconditional repeal.[57] No member of the Pennsylvania delegation took part in the debates, and many were absent or did not vote on numerous occasions. Considering the faithful attendance of the Pennsylvania delegates at the first session of the Tenth Congress and their faithful attendance during the latter part of the second session, their absence might be interpreted as a sign of disinterestedness in, or disgust with, the proceedings. When they did attend and vote, they lent their weight in favor of strong measures and against measures which would result in outright repeal without, at least, a face-saving substitute. The result of this confusion was the passage of the nonintercourse bill on February 27, 1809, by a majority of 81-40. Of the Pennsylvania delegation two were absent and six voted against the bill leaving ten to vote in its favor. Of the six who opposed the measure, three, David Bard, John Porter, and Robert Whitehill, had consistently supported the embargo and enforcement legislation. It can only be assumed that they opposed the nonintercourse bill not because

---

[56] The debate on this bill is scattered between pages 915 and 1026 in the *Annals of Congress,* 10th Cong,. 2d sess.; there are over forty rollcall votes.

[57] The collapse of the Republican majority is excellently summarized in Perkins, *Prologue to War,* 179-83, 225-32.

they favored abandonment of the coercive system but because they viewed it as a bad substitute for the embargo. This was certainly the attitude of the Pennsylvania Republican press.

The Washington *Reporter* was livid at repeal of the embargo and the record of the second session of the Tenth Congress: "Looking back at some of the acts of this session is painful and disgusting." Instead of preserving our honor and independence, "a weak imbicile congress reduc[ed] us to the abject state of colonists." Repeal of the embargo was an act of "submission of the most disgraceful kind." The only legitimate substitute for the embargo was war, but Congress produced a nonintercourse law which would prove to be totally ineffectual. "If the 11th Congress does not 'pluck up the drowned honor' of the nation" we would do best "to submit willingly to colonial status."[58] Duane of the *Aurora* was incensed. Repeal, he believed, resulted from artificial panic created by New England Republicans to whom reelection was more important than the preservation of national rights. The nonintercourse bill would be totally ineffective since those who violated an enforceable embargo would certainly violate this unenforceable measure. On the other hand, Britain, convinced that the United States was too weak and divided to defend its rights by any means, let alone a war, would trample on those rights with increased impertinence.[59]

William Jones, who had supported the embargo wholeheartedly, confident that it would soon be "superseded by measures of dignity and energy," feared that the action of Congress foreshadowed a Federalist triumph. He requested that Republicans be informed of future legislation in order to prepare themselves for their humiliation

[58] Washington *Reporter*, March 13, 1809.
[59] Philadelphia *Aurora*, Feb. 8, Feb. 10, Feb. 12, March 1, March 4, March 7, March 11, March 14, 1809.

as "objects of derision for our credulity."⁶⁰ It is clear that many Pennsylvanians considered nonintercourse a measure of retreat.

The general lack of enthusiasm for the nonintercourse bill among Pennsylvanians reflects more than a willingness to substitute war for embargo. It reflects a very high degree of party loyalty. The ten members of the delegation who voted for the bill were not unaware of the sentiments of their constituents or the attitude of the Republican press. From their earlier support of the embargo, and from their subsequent support of strong measures, it is clear that they supported nonintercourse as a matter of party loyalty, not because they had any faith in the measure. They would have preferred something stronger if they had had a free choice.

The press showed similar loyalty. Condemning the measure as an abandonment of national rights and honor on the one hand, it urged compliance with the measure and continued to pledge support to the administration. At the same time the newspapers pressed for military preparations and continued to demand action to protect America's maritime rights.

In his message to the legislature Governor Snyder expressed regret that "all the measures which the wisdom and anxious patriotism of congress had produced," had failed to win respect for American rights. He hoped, however, the efforts of Congress would meet with general approval and that future efforts would excite "in every American's bosom a fixed and determined resolution to support the general government."⁶¹ Compared to the vigorous approval of the embargo in his earlier message, this endorsement of nonintercourse does little more than damn

⁶⁰ William Jones to William B. Giles (senator from Virginia), Feb. 4, 1809, cited in Higginbotham, *Keystone*, 241.

⁶¹ Governor's Message, Dec. 7, 1809, *Pennsylvania Senate Journal,* 1809-1810, pp. 10-12.

with faint praise. The state legislature, which in the previous session had passed numerous resolutions specifically expressing support for the embargo, passed none in support of nonintercourse, though it did pass some resolutions expressing general support for the policies of the national government.[62] Significantly, these resolutions affirmed a willingness on the part of the General Assembly of Pennsylvania "in the name and on behalf of their constituents" to cooperate with "the general government in all necessary measures" whenever "in the opinion of our national councils, an appeal to the patriotism and force of the American people becomes necessary."[63] The House also passed resolutions approving the conduct of the general government and pledging support in case of an appeal to arms. It indicated its attitude toward nonintercourse by resolving that "continued submission . . . cannot but create a suspicion that all are regardless of our rights, and careless of our fame."[64] Whereas Pennsylvanians had actively supported the embargo because they believed it would be effective, they tolerated nonintercourse not out of conviction, but out of party loyalty.

As the administration moved closer to submission by the adoption of Macon's bill No. 2, Pennsylvania Republicans clung even more tenaciously to the Republican administration. In Congress, the Pennsylvania delegation opposed the measure until the very end, and when it became obvious that it would pass, voted in favor of it. The Republican press condemned the measure more severely than they had condemned nonintercourse. Yet, when President Madison, pursuant to the provisions of the law, reimposed nonintercourse against Britain, the Pennsylvania press stoutly defended his action.

[62] See for example *Pennsylvania Senate Journal*, 1809-1810, pp. 64-68, 104-105; *Pennsylvania House Journal*, 1809-1810, pp. 17-20, 71-73.
[63] *Pennsylvania Senate Journal*, 1809-1810, pp. 104-105.
[64] *Pennsylvania House Journal*, 1809-1810, pp. 65-70, 180-81.

The Eleventh Congress opened its second session in May 1809. Almost immediately a contest developed between a group which wanted to repeal nonintercourse because of its ineffectiveness, and another which admitted the ineffectiveness of nonintercourse but wished to substitute either war or another total embargo. In between was a far larger group which did not know what it wanted. The ensuing debates affirm the observations of Congressman Samuel Taggart of Massachusetts who commented to his friend and pastor: "A more completely divided bewildered, disorganized set of men hardly exists. . . . The Senate and House act in such entire harmony that when one says I will the other says I won't." Senator Gregg wrote to Alexander J. Dallas that "not a single member of Congress . . . appears to have formed a definite opinion as to the course to be pursued."[65] Though an adequate description of Congress, this is not an adequate description of the Pennsylvania delegation.

The debate on Macon's proposals is long and infinitely more complex than on the embargo or nonintercourse bills. Nothing of great value would be learned by tracing it minutely through both houses of Congress. In each house there were numerous amendments and a great deal of parliamentary maneuvering. The result was the passage by each house of totally different measures. After repeated conference committee recommendations had been rejected, both houses adopted the measure substantially as it had been originally proposed. The bill opened trade with both belligerents and provided, in effect, that if France repealed her decrees as they affected the United States, the president would reimpose nonintercourse

[65] Samuel Taggart to Rev. John Taylor, April 27, 1810, in "Letters of Samuel Taggart, Representative in Congress, 1803-1814," ed. George Haynes, American Antiquarian Society, *Proceedings*, new series, XXXIII, 347; Andrew Gregg to A. J. Dallas, Dec. 4, 1809, Dallas Papers, Historical Society of Pennsylvania.

against Britain. Likewise, if Britain repealed her orders, the United States would reimpose nonintercourse against France. In the more than fifty rollcalls that were taken during the debate, the Pennsylvania delegation showed remarkable consistency. Fourteen of the members voted in favor of every amendment which would have put teeth into the measure—amendments to double duties on goods imported from either belligerent, amendments to allow merchant ships to travel in convoys and arm in self defense, amendments to prohibit French and British vessels from entering American waters. Two members, William Milnor and Robert Jenkins, always opposed the strengthening amendments. Daniel Hiester and Samuel Smith wavered, but sided much more regularly with Milnor and Jenkins. On the final passage of Macon's bill No. 2 the Pennsylvania delegation divided 10-7-1. Jenkins and Milnor opposed, while Samuel Smith and Hiester who generally voted with them supported the measure. William Anderson and Adam Seybert, new members from Philadelphia, David Bard, William Crawford, newly elected from Gettysburg, and John Ross—all of whom had supported strong measures and all of whom, except Ross who did not run again, later voted for war in the Twelfth Congress, voted against the bill. Of these, Ross, Anderson, and Seybert participated in the debate. They supported Senate amendments providing for the arming of merchant ships because, according to Ross, the measure as passed by the House was not calculated to assert the honor and dignity of the nation.[66] In a second speech Ross asserted that only three courses were open to the nation. It must abandon commerce, suffer England to regulate it, or protect it by force. The first two courses, he argued, were dishonorable and Macon's bill did not provide for energetic measures. It was, in fact, nothing more than a "third edition" of the

[66] *Annals of Congress,* 11th Cong., 2d sess., 1267-73, 1441.

embargo based on the dishonorable principle that the best way to protect the nation's rights and commerce is to abandon them. America's experience with policy based on this principle proved that it was futile. It had not induced either belligerent to modify its policy. The United States suffered intolerable insults at the hands of the British, he concluded, and the time had come to abandon the principle of the embargo and to undertake strong measures. "I am for manly resistance and for declaring in our laws as well as speeches that the embargo ground is no longer tenable and that this nation will defend its rights, by force if necessary."

Adam Seybert supported amendments imposing a heavy duty on British and French goods to give some measure of strength to a bill that otherwise dishonored the nation, and on the ground that such duties would foster infant industry.[67]

William Anderson opposed the bill because it entailed an abject surrender of the nation's rights, honor, and independence. Those who supported the bill on the supposition that it would avert war, he maintained, were grossly mistaken. Submission to insult leads only to greater injury. American experience had shown that peaceful and conciliatory measures on its part did not bring forth similar measures from Great Britain. On the contrary, the British cabinet read such measures as signs of weakness and was prompted into even more insulting measures. "I do myself deprecate war, and am as desirous of peace as any gentleman on the floor," he said, but rather than agree to this measure which can only be viewed as complete submission, he would "grant letters of marque and reprisal," and if necessary go further. "I would call forth the resources of the nation, present a firm front, sustain our honor, defend our rights and independence and not suffer them

[67] *Annals of Congress,* 11th Cong., 2d sess., 1891-1900.

tamely to fall at the feet of a tyrant without a struggle."[68]
It can only be assumed that these four Republicans who
opposed the measure felt it was too weak and agreed with
Thomas Gholson of Virginia who declared that the bill
"held up the honor and character of this nation to the
highest bidder."[69] On the other hand, Smilie, who asserted
that this bill is "on all hands . . . acknowledged to be
submission" and who favored letting the nonintercourse
bill expire without any substitute in preference to passing
Macon's bill, voted for it.[70] Defending his about-face,
Smilie observed that the House was divided into three
groups: those who would do nothing, those who preferred
"more energetic measures," among whom he counted himself, and those who wished to follow a moderate course
by passing Macon's bill. Those who favored energetic
measures, he argued, would gain nothing by allying themselves with those who would do nothing. On the other
hand, by supporting the bill they gained time, gave Great
Britain one more chance to change her policy, and did
not deny themselves the possibility of supporting stronger
measures in the future.[71] The only plausible explanation
for this otherwise unexplainable behavior of Pennsylvania's Republican delegation is that to some, party regularity was a primary consideration, while others were
willing to abandon the party standard to show their dissatisfaction with the administration's submissive policy.
The fact that four of the Republican defectors were newly
elected congressmen to whom the necessity for party
regularity might not have become obvious lends some
credibility to this conjecture.

The press hardly took any notice of the passage of
Macon's bill No. 2. The text of the law was printed in

68 *Annals of Congress*, 11th Cong., 2d sess., 1325-28.
69 Ibid., 1772.
70 Ibid., 1643.
71 Ibid., 1188-89.

all the Republican papers within two weeks of passage, but the editors on the whole were silent. In February 1811, almost a year after the bill was passed, Duane reviewed the course of American policy which had brought us to "this unhappy state." In his summary he argued that under the circumstances, the embargo was the best policy that could have been adopted because it was a substitute for war. It would have achieved its intended goals if it had been continued, but a weak-willed administration had abandoned it for a course which led ultimately to total submission.[72]

Macon's bill No. 2 set the scene for one of the most embarrassing and tangled diplomatic farces in the nation's early history. On August 5, 1810, President Madison received a note from the French foreign minister, the Duc de Cadore, asserting that the French decrees, as they applid to American commerce, would be repealed as of the following November, if by that time Britain had repealed her orders, or the United States, in compliance with Macon's bill, had reimposed nonintercourse against Great Britain. When Congress passed Macon's bill it had not contemplated the possibility of such a conditional repeal of either belligerent's restrictive regulations. Although the bill provided that the president must have concrete evidence of repeal, it did not specify what satisfactory evidence was. Madison's acceptance of the Cadore letter at its face value led to charges of Francophilia, or more charitably, that he had allowed himself to be duped. The two most recent studies convincingly dispute these allegations. Irving Brant and Bradford Perkins contend that Madison was fully aware of the pitfalls of the French proposal, but decided to accept it in the hope of forcing England to repeal her orders.[73]

[72] Philadelphia *Aurora*, Feb. 7, 1811.
[73] Brant, *Madison: The President, 1809-1812*, pp. 207-21; Perkins, *Prologue*, 246-53.

Whatever his motives, on November 2, 1810, Madison issued a proclamation stating that France had met the requirements of Macon's bill. If England did not revoke its edicts within three months, nonintercourse would be revived.[74] When England took no action, trade with that nation was closed on February 2, 1811.

Pennsylvania Federalists were incensed by what they considered Madison's capitulation to France. Almost daily, articles in both the Pennsylvania *Gazette* and the Pittsburgh *Gazette* attempted to show that the French decrees had not been revoked. These articles generally contained letters or reports from sailors and ship captains who claimed they had been molested by the French since the announced date of repeal. These "proofs" are generally followed by statements to the effect that the administration must be dominated by French influence and that the purpose of economic coercion was to destroy commerce and vent the administration's hatred of England.[75] The Pennsylvania *Gazette* also carried many articles on the progress of British manufactures. These began in the spring of 1810 and appeared often and in ever increasing detail until the end of February 1812. These features appear without comment, but are so conspicuous that one begins to wonder why they are included. The reason becomes obvious on October 30, 1811, in an article introducing excerpts from an English pamphlet reporting the progress of manufactures there. "The positive, and sometimes avowed object of the present rulers of the U. S. in their suicidal measures . . . having been to annihilate British manufactures and impoverish Britain; and Congress about to convene to witness the effects of these measures and contemplate new ones," the *Gazette* pub-

---

[74] *American State Papers: Foreign Affairs*, III, 392.
[75] Pennsylvania *Gazette*, Oct. 23, Nov. 6, Nov. 13, 1811, Jan. 8, Feb. 5, 1812; Pittsburgh *Gazette*, Oct. 17, Oct. 24, Nov. 9, Nov. 19, Dec. 4, Dec. 11, Dec. 17, 1811, Jan. 16, Jan. 23, Feb. 6, 1812.

lished the fact of British progress to show that American policy had been ineffective and that similar efforts in the future would be equally unavailing.[76]

The Republican press rallied to the administration, and stoutly defended Madison's policy of accepting Cadore's note as evidence of French repeal and of reviving non-intercourse against Britain. The *Aurora* strongly supported Madison's policy, though it had not particularly favored Macon's bill. The French, Duane asserted, had "unquestionably repealed their decrees" on the condition proposed. "The condition is that we shall cease to import from Great Britain. . . . The law is clear and explicit and admits of no equivocation or alternation." By its very nature, Duane continued, Macon's bill is different from "normal domestic legislation which may be repealed or amended at pleasure. . . . The law is in fact, a convention with a foreign nation . . . and its execution is . . . as obligatory on our government as the most solemn treaty."[77] If the United States were to keep its word, "not one iota of merchandise from Great Britain or her dependencies can be admitted into the United States." In the past two years the progress of American manufactures "is not only incalculable but . . . incredible." Affirmation and continued application of policies that would force Americans to rely on domestic production would "in a few years . . . place us in a situation really independent of all the nations of the earth."[78] The Carlisle *Gazette* followed the same theme. The president had proclaimed that the French had revoked their decrees and in compliance with our own laws had revived nonintercourse against Britain. Macon's bill could not be amended because if "we once deviate from a compact, we lose our standing in the affairs of

[76] Pennsylvania *Gazette*, Oct. 30, 1811.
[77] Philadelphia *Aurora*, Jan. 9, Jan. 14, Jan. 23, 1811.
[78] Philadelphia *Aurora*, Aug. 1, 1811.

nations."[79] Furthermore, Britain's policy toward the United States since French repeal exhibited "a mean, fraudulent, low, cunning" attitude. Britain had justified the orders-in-council on the grounds of retaliation, but now that the French had repealed their decrees, the British refused to repeal their orders. The real reason for the British orders was their fear of American development in commerce and manufacturing. Their goal was to stop that growth before we became too serious competitors. How ironic that the very policy they followed had the opposite effect.[80]

In his message to the legislature, the governor observed that "it is a matter of satisfaction to perceive that one of the belligerents has evinced a disposition to respect our neutral rights. . . . On the part of the other belligerent hardly a symptom appears to warrant an expectation of an amiable adjustment." The message concluded by again pledging Pennsylvania's support if the government were to decide that only force could secure the nation's rights.[81] The *Commonwealth* praised the governor's speech for expressing "that patriotic support of the general government so often wanting among public men." The paper carried many articles about smuggling across the Canadian border, exulting whenever the merchandise was confiscated. "This is as it should be—the laws ought to be rigidly enforced."[82]

One correspondent expressed another theme that could be found regularly in the press. One of the impediments to forceful action had been the problem of whether we should wage war against all our assailants, or single out

[79] Carlisle *Gazette,* March 3, 1811.
[80] Carlisle *Gazette,* Aug. 23, 1811.
[81] Governor's message, Dec. 6, 1811, quoted in the Pittsburgh *Commonwealth,* Dec. 16, 1811.
[82] Pittsburgh *Commonwealth,* Oct. 28, Nov. 4, Dec. 16, 1811, Feb. 11, March 24, 1812.

one enemy. That problem no longer existed. Napoleon's repeal of the French decrees had settled outstanding differences between the United States and France. England, however, persisted in her outrageous demands, refused to do this nation justice, and continued her usurpations. She was now the only enemy and America's "independence, honor and patriotism demand satisfaction."[83]

Reverting to its traditional 13-2-3 division, the Pennsylvania delegation voted with the majority in Congress to deny all appeals for permission to import goods loaded or paid for before the president's proclamation, or before the reimposition of nonintercourse.[84]

In the debate on the actions taken pursuant to Macon's bill No. 2, Pennsylvania Republicans affirmed their attachment to the principle of commercial coercion, but more particularly to the Republican administration. Having supported the embargo as an honorable alternative to war, they had acquiesced in the substitution of nonintercourse which, all agreed, was a much weaker measure. With less unanimity they had supported the even weaker policy of Macon's bill No. 2. When that policy came under bitter Federalist attack—an attack much more legitimate than the assault on the earlier policies of the Republican administration—Republicans rallied stoutly to support the policy and the administration which pursued it although most of them had not approved of the policy and would have preferred a substitution of war for nonintercourse.

The people of the state affirmed their support of the administration and their desires for stronger measures by their votes in the elections for the Twelfth Congress. William Milnor and Daniel Hiester, who had always voted differently from the rest of the delegation, and Samuel Smith and Robert Jenkins, who had often sided with them,

---

[83] "My Voice Is Still for War," Philadelphia *Aurora*, Sept. 9, 1811.
[84] *Annals of Congress*, 11th Cong., 1st and 2d sess., 232, 441, 446, 1354.

were not reelected. In their place Pennsylvania Republicans sent Jonathan Roberts, Roger Davis, Abner Lacock, and William Piper, all of whom supported every move toward war in the Twelfth Congress. One congressional election is particularly instructive. Matthias Richards, who had served in the Tenth and Eleventh Congresses as a representative of a dissident Republican faction in Pennsylvania, was renominated by them in 1810. Regular Republicans put up their own candidate. The Federalists also put up a man. In September Richards publicly withdrew his name, stating that a Republican split in the three-county district he represented might result in the election of three Federalists. Since all Republicans voted the same on national issues he felt he could prevent an intraparty fight by dropping out of the race.[85] Richards' resignation in the interest of party harmony indicates that public sentiment was running in that direction. The final election results certainly reflect this sentiment. Of the eighteen representatives all but one were Republican and none of these had run on the platform or as the candidate of the state's dissident Republican faction. In the face of grave national problems the state Republican party, often divided on state issues, united to send to Congress a "pure" Republican delegation. In the elections for the state legislature, the results were equally indicative of the sentiment for party unity. The state House numbered seventy-two Republicans, seventeen Federalists, and six "nondescripts"; the senate, twenty-one Republicans, seven Federalists, and three "nondescripts."[86]

[85] Philadelphia *Aurora*, Sept. 22, 1810. Higginbotham, *Keystone*, 219.
[86] J.M.S. "General Abner Lacock," *Pennsylvania Magazine of History and Biography*, IV (1880), 202-209; William A. Russ, "Trends in the Pennsylvania Congressional Delegations," *Pennsylvania History*, X (October, 1943), 268-81; Binns to Roberts, Oct. 3, 1810, Roberts Papers; Philadelphia *Aurora*, Oct. 5, Oct. 10, 1810; Pittsburgh *Commonwealth*, July 2, Sept. 3, Sept. 10, Sept. 17, Sept. 24, Oct. 19, 1810; Higginbotham, *Keystone*, 220.

Pennsylvania's Republican congressmen could have little doubt as to what was expected of them. The same papers that had defended the administration's policies against Federalist attacks urged the new Congress to adopt a more vigorous policy. Shortly after it opened its first session, the Twelfth Congress received a series of resolutions passed by the Pennsylvania legislature affirming that British policy "cannot but arouse the virtuous indignation of every friend of this nation"; that "when submission or resistance to the unjust demands of a tyrant are the alternative, the latter only can be chosen by the free men of America"; that in order to "repel aggression and obtain reparations [we will] vigorously exert all the powers which we possess to accelerate the accomplishments of such military preparations as the wisdom of the national legislature may require." They concluded by pledging to support "an appeal to arms . . . at the risk of our lives and fortune."[87]

The attitude of the press is typified by one statement from the Pittsburgh *Commonwealth*: "Submission or resistance seems to be our inevitable lot. And we should blush for the spirit of our country if a sentiment favorable to the former were suffered to be admitted to our councils. As to the mongorl [*sic*] state of resisting only on paper . . . we believe the public heartily tired of it and fully ready for change." Preparations therefore must be made for war. England would then repeal or modify her orders. If not, "hostilities must ensue."[88]

Pennsylvania's Republican congressmen did not disappoint their constituents. During the Twelfth Congress they supported all preparatory measures, except some efforts to strengthen the navy, and ultimately cast sixteen votes for war. It seems quite clear that from the time

[87] *Annals of Congress*, 12th Cong., 1st sess., 586-88.
[88] Pittsburgh *Commonwealth*, Jan. 7, 1812.

Jefferson proposed the first embargo as an alternative to war, until Madison proposed the embargo of April 1812 as a precursor to war, Pennsylvania Republicans whole-heartedly supported the administration even though they did not always approve of the substitutes for war which followed the original embargo. The divisions in the state's congressional delegation, the results of congressional elections, and the attitudes of the press indicate quite clearly that the state's support of the ineffectual efforts at commercial coercion which followed the embargo were based not on faith in the effectiveness of the policies, but on loyalty to the Republican party.

One other factor helps to explain Pennsylvania's support for the policy of commercial restriction: the belief that this policy would enhance the development of the state's manufacturing. Alone, this factor would not have won support for the policy, but it undoubtedly reinforced the support given as a matter of party loyalty. The extent to which the commercial policy of the administration and the subsequent war influenced the development of domestic manufactures is the subject of some controversy, but there is much evidence to corroborate Victor Clark's generalization that "the isolation of the Republic during the period of non-intercourse and the war of 1812 stimulated factory industry."[89]

All of the standard statistical compendia include charts showing significant increases in the volume and value of domestic manufactures between 1807 and 1815.[90] Rather than reproduce facts and figures culled from these works

[89] Victor Clark, *History of Manufactures in the United States, 1807-1860* (Washington, 1916), 235.
[90] See Timothy Pitkin, *Statistical View of the Congress of the United States of America* (New Haven, 1835), 261-62, 266-92, 302, 305; Anne Bezanson, Robert Gray, and Miriam Hussey, *Wholesale Prices in Philadelphia, 1784-1861* (Philadelphia, 1936); Arthur Cole, *Wholesale Commodity Prices in the United States, 1700-1861* (Cambridge, 1938), 25-40, 138-49.

which were themselves compiled long after the event, the following paragraphs will present evidence, admittedly impressionistic, to show that many contemporary Pennsylvanians believed the commercial policy of the government to be beneficial.

In his report on manufacturers in 1810 Gallatin declared that the interference of the belligerents with American neutral trade and the commercial policy of the general government had "broken inveterate habits and given a general impulse to which must be ascribed the general increase of manufactures during the last two years." Capital and industry had been forced into other channels by this policy resulting in the increases he reported.[91]

The press and people of Pennsylvania seem to have accepted Gallatin's propositions. The United States *Gazette,* a Federalist newspaper which might be expected to describe the effects of the embargo in the worst possible light, admitted that the overall effects for manufacturing were beneficial. It described in detail the sufferings of sailors and their families and of other groups which were adversely affected by the embargo, but concluded that "the Embargo has as yet produced *comparatively* little inconvenience in this city and neighborhood." While the winter had been hard, heavy construction provided jobs for eight or ten thousand men who had been thrown out of work by the embargo.[92] The United States *Gazette* predicted a hard winter when frost ended the building boom, but gloried in the building boom of the summer.[93] The Philadelphia *Price Current,* a Republican paper, was even more direct. It published a lengthy article on Philadelphia manufactures "to prove that by the President's originating partial depravations, he had ultimately

[91] *American State Papers: Finance,* II, 430.
[92] United States *Gazette,* Oct. 8, 1808.
[93] Ibid., Oct. 22, 1808.

bestowed on his country immense and imperishable benefits."[94]

Shortly after the embargo was passed, Duane defended it on the grounds of its expected domestic effect. The measure, he said, would be a "wall of fire" behind which the United States could establish manufactures, develop its resources, develop means of internal transportation, and thus establish "that independence which is now only nominal." He called America's dependence on foreign commerce "a great curse" but said that now there is a golden opportunity to dispense with it by promoting domestic industries.[95] Assessing the effects of the embargo a year later, Duane asserted that "it greatly helped the development of manufactures to a degree yet unknown." He proclaimed that "the embargo has built or nearly built 10,000 houses in this city. The embargo has erected two manufactories [*sic*] of shot . . . which forever secures the circulation at home of about two hundred thousand dollars, hitherto sent abroad to pay for shot."[96] Duane relied heavily on this argument. The embargo promoted manufactures not only because it forced Americans to rely on their own resources, but because it kept American capital at home. "The capital of merchants and monied men being withdrawn from commerce, has been appropriated to other purposes."[97] At a dinner given in Carlisle to celebrate "the improved prospects" for industry, the diners celebrated the increase in manufactures and the embargo by drinking a toast to "the best mode of warfare for our country—the artillery of carding and spinning and the musketry of shuttles and sledges."[98]

Addresses by the governor to the state legislature reflect

[94] Philadelphia *Price Current,* Oct. 25, 1808.
[95] *Aurora,* Jan. 6, 1808.
[96] Philadelphia *Aurora,* Sept. 1, 1808.
[97] Philadelphia *Aurora,* Nov. 3, 1808.
[98] Carlisle *Gazette,* Nov. 15, 1808.

the same belief. In his message to the nineteenth session of that body, Snyder admitted that the embargo had caused some distress, but the temporary hardships were not to be compared to the long-range benefits. The embargo, he argued, "by forcing us to rely on our own resources has accelerated the development of domestic manufactures which will provide that economic independence without which political independence cannot endure."[99]

The Pennsylvania house responded by passing resolutions, with Federalist support, promising to use only items of domestic manufactures and by appointing a committee to consider what the state could do to aid manufactures. The same body passed a bill appropriating money "to relieve the distress of the seamen of Philadelphia" who had been deprived "of support and employ by the embargo."[100]

The following year Governor Snyder observed with satisfaction that "in proportion to the difficulty of access to, and commerce with, foreign nations, is the zeal and exertion to supply our wants by home manufactures. Our mills and furnaces are greatly multiplied; new beds of ore have been discovered, and the industry and enterprise of our citizens are turning them to the most useful purposes. Many new and highly valuable industries have been established, and we now make in Pennsylvania various articles of domestic use, for which, two years since, we were wholly dependent upon foreign nations." After listing specific factories that had been established throughout the state, Snyder recommended to the legislature that it "devise means to encourage domestic manufactures."[101] In 1811 Snyder praised the skill and enterprise of the

[99] *Pennsylvania House Journal,* 19th sess., 1808-1809, pp. 19-22.
[100] Ibid., 144, 187, 211.
[101] *Pennsylvania Senate Journal,* 20th sess., 1809-1810, pp. 10-12.

artisans of the state who had "turned the potential economic chaos which might have been expected due to the embarrassing state of our foreign relations to a great advantage" for the state by weaning Pennsylvanians from foreign commercial speculation and inviting their attention to the exploration of the internal resources of their state. This, he added, would lead to a great expansion of domestic manufacturing which in turn would convert the "transient calamity into a permanent, substantial national advantage."[102]

Individuals attested to a similar belief. William Dalzell complimented Jefferson on the embargo which made possible rapid industrial growth on every hand, and expressed the hope that Congress would enact other legislation to protect and encourage American industrial development.[103]

While not explicitly supporting the embargo, Nicholas Biddle gives an interesting account of the general indifference to the measure by men of wealth. "You would hardly recognize Philadelphia, so much has it grown and improved," he wrote to a friend in Paris. "Your former acquaintances are here and prospering." Commenting on the political effects of the embargo, Biddle mentioned that it probably caused the larger Federalist vote in New England, and some other areas, but significantly does not mention Philadelphia or Pennsylvania. He concludes, "in all these matters I do not mingle. . . . I am occupying myself with my profession."[104]

A delegation of merchants and laborers wrote Jefferson: "We behold in a temporary suspension of our commerce

[102] The governor's message is cited in Niles *Register*, Dec. 21, 1811, pp. 281-84.
[103] Dalzell to Jefferson, Feb. 10, 1809; Short to Jefferson, Aug. 27, 1808, expresses the same sentiment. Both letters are cited in L. M. Sears, *Jefferson and the Embargo* (Durham, 1927), 216-19.
[104] Biddle to La Grange, Sept. 26, 1808, cited in Sears, *Jefferson*, 218.

an ephemeral and doubtful evil, producing a great growing and lasting good. We see arising out of this cause the
prolific sources of our internal wealth explored and with
industry and ability directed through channels which . . .
enrich our country with solid wealth and make her more
independent and wealthy."[105] Jefferson responded by
thanking them for their support and commending them
for their farsightedness in seeing the long range benefits
that might derive.[106]

Charles Ingersoll's description of Philadelphia provides
an excellent insight into contemporary attitudes:

> Who walks the street of Philadelphia, and sees, not-
> withstanding, a twelve-month stagnation of trade,
> several hundred substantial and elegant houses build-
> ing, and the labouring community employed at good
> wages, who reads at every corner advertisements for
> workmen for factories of glass, of shot, of arms, of ho-
> siery and coarse cloths, of pottery and many other
> goods and wares; who finds that within the last year
> rents have risen one-third and that houses are hardly to
> be had at these prices, . . . in a word, who perceives,
> wherever he goes, the bustle of industry and the smile
> of content; who, under such circumstances, that is not
> too stupid to perceive and too prejudiced to believe
> when he does perceive, can doubt the solid capital of
> this country?[107]

When added to the evidence denying depression presented earlier in this study, these comments suggest
strongly that Pennsylvanians were greatly interested in

[105] Delegates of the Democratic Republicans of the City of Philadelphia to Thomas Jefferson, March 1, 1808. The letter is found in the
Philadelphia *Aurora* for March 4, 1808.

[106] Jefferson to Democratic Citizens, March 20, 1808, *Jefferson Writings* (Lipscomb edition), XII, 17.

[107] Charles J. Ingersoll, *A View of the Rights and Wrongs, Power and
Policy of the United States of America* (Philadelphia, 1808), 49.

the development of domestic manufactures and believed that the embargo was a positive measure to that end. The acceptance of commercial coercion as a viable alternative to war; the sense of party loyalty which led Pennsylvanians to continue supporting measures of commercial coercion when it had become obvious that they were no longer alternatives to war but substitutes for action; and the belief that long range economic benefits would accrue to the state and the nation from the policy explain to a large extent the state's support for the commercial policy of the Republican administrations.

CHAPTER FIVE

Party Solidarity as
a Motive for War

The policy of commercial coercion, whatever its domestic effects, did not achieve the intended result. British and French violations of American neutral rights continued without abatement. Moreover, the changes in the method of commercial coercion were beginning to convince many people that the purposes for which the policy had been initiated had changed. The embargo of 1807 had been proposed as an alternative to war. The people had accepted it as such and defended it on the ground that it was a forceful measure. Macon's bill No. 2 seemed more a substitute for action, a face-saving device designed to appease domestic opposition and to give the appearance of having done something while in reality doing very little. Those Americans who felt that the nation should effectively protect its rights concluded that the measure had humiliated their country.[1]

In the months between the adjournment of the Eleventh Congress and the embargo of April 1812, there occurred a noticeable change in public attitudes. Pennsylvania newspaper opinion, the attitude of leading Republicans in the state, and the composition of the state's delegation to Congress indicate clearly that all had concluded that commercial coercion had failed; only two alternatives remained—war or submission, and only the former was acceptable.

In the summer and fall of 1811, the state's Republican newspapers were filled with denunciations of the policies of the Eleventh Congress, condemnations of Federalists to whom they attributed both the failure to reach an agreement with England and the failure of Congress to take forceful action to protect American rights, and demands that the new Congress "stop debating and act." Reviewing the proceedings of the Eleventh Congress, William Duane was unhappy with the result. "We wish that they had followed a different course. It should have been an energetic course, and should, ere this, have issued in peace or war." Congress had not followed such a course, Duane contended, because "Anglo-men" had successfully diverted its attention. By preventing Congress from taking necessary action in national affairs, these men "hoped to destroy public confidence in our government." Once this was achieved "federalism or something quite as bad will soon follow." The next Congress should not allow its attention to be diverted. It must take energetic action to preserve American rights and thus restore "the confidence of the people in their government," and respect in the world for republican institutions.[2]

The editor of the Carlisle *Gazette* argued that the publication of Federalist newspapers which "give the British government the impression that we are divided at home and therefore cannot act vigorously abroad" had foiled all efforts to reach an agreement with that country. If war

---

[1] Bradford Perkins' chapter dealing with the actions of the Eleventh Congress which passed Macon's bill No. 2 is aptly entitled "America's Humiliation"; *Prologue to War* (Berkeley, 1961), chapter seven, 223-60. See also D. R. Anderson, "Insurgents of 1811," American Historical Association, *Annual Report,* I (1911), 167-76.

[2] Philadelphia *Aurora,* April 6, 1811.

should result, Federalists would have no one but themselves to blame. Taking a slightly different approach, the Pittsburgh *Commonwealth* contended that Federalist opposition to effective measures short of war had forced this nation to its present position, and that "there is now no alternative to war or submission."[3] The Philadelphia *Aurora* proclaimed that "the time has come to do away with party disputes and unite behind the government for self-preservation." Continuance of the present policy "will lead to the complete disgrace of America."

Like most other Republican papers, the *Aurora* covered the clash between the *President* and the *Little Belt* in great detail. It drew from the incident the obvious lesson that forceful action was much more effective than negotiation. But it drew another lesson that, in Duane's mind, was much more important. The public's favorable reaction to the clash, Duane asserted, was proof that the people would support the government if it would take firm action to protect the nation's rights.[4]

It was against this background that Pennsylvania congressmen left for Washington in October 1811. The Pennsylvania delegation to the Twelfth Congress contained eight new members. With the exception of the delegations sent to the Second and Fourth congresses this was the highest percentage of new members in any Pennsylvania delegation prior to the War of 1812. Taking into consideration the increases in the size of the delegation, this was also the highest percentage of new members until 1832.[5] More significant than the size of the change was the nature of the change. Joseph Hiester, Robert

[3] Carlisle *Gazette*, Aug. 16, Oct. 7, 1811; Pittsburgh *Commonwealth*, July 11, 1811.

[4] Philadelphia *Aurora*, May 27, June 3, June 6, June 9, Aug. 8, Sept. 19, Sept. 21, Sept. 23, 1811. See also Dauphin *Guardian*, June 4, 1810, July 12, 1811.

[5] William A. Russ, "Trends in Pennsylvania's Congressional Delegations," *Pennsylvania History*, X (October 1943), 282.

Jenkins, William Milnor, and Samuel Smith, all of whom had voted so often with the minority in the Eleventh Congress were defeated. John Rea and Matthias Richards, who had generally supported the administration, did not run. Of the new members, all but James Milnor were Republicans, and all but he and William Rodman were warm supporters of the administration, and ultimately all but those two joined the rest of the delegation in voting for war.[6]

Not much is known about all the new members, but what is known indicates clearly that the basic issues in the election were the necessity for vigorous action by the government and the candidates' willingness to support the administration. Discussing the forthcoming state elections, a correspondent who signed himself "My Voice Is Still for War" argued that it was essential for the safety and honor of the nation to return large Republican majorities both to the state house and to Congress. "There is a certain class," he claimed, "who express a contempt for the nature of our government. It is calculated, so they say, only for smooth water and favorable gales:—but when the surge rises and the tempest roars it will be dashed on the rocks or swallowed in the quicksands." This was not true. It was this class of men who had prevented the government from taking effective action in the past because they "place profit above liberty." Elect a Congress founded in public sentiment and the nation's enemies, at home and abroad, would see that Americans would willingly endure the hardships of war. They "will regard no expense when liberty is at stake."[7]

Two contests underline these issues. In an eight-county

[6] The election of 1810 is discussed, but very unsatisfactorily in chapter nine of Sanford Higginbotham, *Keystone of the Democratic Arch* (Harrisburg, 1952), 213-20.

[7] Philadelphia *Aurora*, Sept. 25, 1811. This letter is widely reprinted in the Republican newspapers of the state.

district in western Pennsylvania, which had been represented by Samuel Smith in the Tenth and Eleventh congresses, a warm contest developed between Abner Lacock
and Adamson Tannehill, both Republicans. Smith's constant opposition to administration measures had aroused
so much opposition that he was not renominated.[8] The
major issue in the nominations of Lacock and Tannehill
was whether Allegheny County, the most populous county
in the district, should have a preponderant voice in the
nomination of the district's congressmen or whether all
the counties should have an equal voice. Unable to
settle the issue, both men were presented to the people.
Tannehill was nominated by Allegheny County Republicans, Lacock, by a Republican convention called by the
other seven counties. The election turned on the men's
support for vigorous measures and their party regularity.
The Republican press in the area, including the newspapers of Allegheny County supported Lacock because
of the strong proadministration position he had taken as
a member of the state legislature. They also cited his
efforts on behalf of militia reform. The Federalists did
not put up a candidate. There was some mention of
supporting Smith, but nothing came of it. In September
the Federalist Pittsburgh *Gazette* destroyed whatever
chance Tannehill might have had by coming out in his
favor. Abner Lacock carried every county in the district
except Allegheny and won the House seat by over four
hundred votes. Elected as a "war candidate," Lacock
while in Congress "took a bold stand for war measures . . .
and stood nobly by the Democratic administration of
James Madison."[9]

[8] For attacks on Smith see Pittsburgh *Commonwealth*, Aug. 7, Aug.
14, Sept. 19, Sept. 26, Oct. 3, 1810; Washington *Reporter*, July 9, July
16, Aug. 1, Aug. 8, 1810. These papers also carry attacks on Smith
from other newspapers in the district.

[9] J.M.S., "General Abner Lacock," *Pennsylvania Magazine of History*

In the three-county district made up of Chester, Lancaster, and Berks counties Republican factionalism resulted in the nomination of two Republicans, the incumbent Matthias Richards and John Hyneman. When the Federalists put up a candidate of their own, Richards withdrew from the contest. In a public letter reprinted in the *Aurora* Richards explained his withdrawal by pointing out that a division in Republican ranks might result in the election of Federalist candidates which would be bad for the country. Since all Republicans voted the same on national issues, and since it was important that administration forces have a large majority in Congress, he felt he should drop out of the race to assure a Republican victory.[10] The virtually unanimous support which the other new Republican congressmen gave to the administration in the Twelfth Congress indicates that similar considerations prompted their nomination and election.

When Congress met in November 1811, there was no general agreement on what policy should be followed. "The House wants men to take the lead," Jonathan Roberts wrote to his brother. He did not know "whether to say we shall have bold and great measures or not." The president's message urging Congress to put the United States in "an armor and an attitude demanded by the crisis" pleased Roberts, but what he considered congressional tardiness infuriated him: "We have been four days in session and the whole business has been the organization of the House, receiving the message and documents and appointing one standing committee." For him such delay was impossible. The president's message "is as

and Biography, IV (1880), 202-209. The discussion of this election is based on a close reading of the Pittsburgh *Commonwealth,* the Pittsburgh *Mercury,* the Pittsburgh *Gazette,* and the Washington *Reporter* for the summer and fall of 1810. See also Harry Houtz, "Abner Lacock," *Western Pennsylvania Historical Magazine,* XXII (1939), 171-87.

10 Philadelphia *Aurora,* Sept. 26, 1810.

important as could have been anticipated and yet we throw away a day before the smallest step is taken to put it in a train of consideration."[11]

Roberts's strictures were too harsh. The time which to him seemed wasted was put to good use by the war-minded men who had been elected to the Twelfth Congress. At a Republican caucus on November 3 these men, commonly dubbed "war hawks," nominated Henry Clay of Kentucky as Speaker of the House. The following day Clay, who had made a reputation as a war man while sitting in the Senate in the previous session, was elected Speaker by a vote of 75 to 44. Pennsylvania Republicans provided 15 votes for him, and none voted against him.[12] Clay used his position to assure that the House would act favorably on the president's recommendations. He packed the important committees with war hawk majorities, and appointed prominent war hawks to the chairmanship of the important Foreign Affairs, Military Affairs, Naval Affairs, and Ways and Means committees.

While the Foreign Affairs Committee considered the president's message, Republicans in Pennsylvania praised the manly attitude it displayed and urged Congress to act quickly, favorably, and decisively on his recommendations. It was intended "to redeem the public mind from despondence and restore the nation to confidence in itself and faith in its government," wrote Duane. Congress must quickly decide upon action to implement the president's message, "or resign itself to submission."[13] Governor Snyder praised the president's message in his opening speech to the state legislature and urged the members to prepare the militia for impending hostilities.

[11] Jonathan Roberts to Matthew Roberts, Nov. 9, Nov. 11, 1811, Roberts Papers.
[12] *Annals of Congress*, 12th Cong., 1st sess., 330. Bernard Mayo, *Henry Clay, Spokesman of the New West* (Boston, 1937).
[13] Philadelphia *Aurora*, Nov. 7, 1811; Washington *Reporter*, Nov. 13, 1811.

He pledged the support of Pennsylvania should the government find it necessary to wage war to support the "honor and independence of our beloved country." James Milnor, the only Federalist in the Pennsylvania delegation, hoped that the federal paper in Philadelphia would not adopt the tone of those in Boston, because that would prompt Republicans to even greater efforts to enact the president's proposals.[14]

On November 29, the Foreign Affairs Committee submitted its report. Stating that the period had arrived when "it is the sacred duty of Congress to call forth the patriotism and resources of the country," the committee condemned Britain's past hostilities and recommended war preparations. These included bringing the regular army to full strength, raising fifty thousand additional volunteers, arming merchantmen and outfitting existing warships.[15] In the voting on the resolutions of the Foreign Affairs Committee, the Pennsylvania delegation was virtually unanimous. There were five resolutions presented. On four of them not one Pennsylvania representative cast a negative vote. Robert Brown, John Smilie, Robert Whitehill, and William Rodman voted against the fifth resolution asking the president to put existing naval vessels into commission.

Roberts was quite satisfied. The committee's proposals "will go into effect and they must speedily lead to war," he wrote to his brother the day after the report was submitted. A week later he was even more certain. "Congress will declare war against Britain if she does not do us justice before we rise. I shall vote for it."[16] The Pennsylvania delegation solidly supported the committee re-

14 *Pennsylvania Archives,* 4th series, IV, 746-49; James Milnor to S. Bradford, Dec. 10, 1811, Bradford Collection, Historical Society of Pennsylvania.

15 *Annals of Congress,* 12th Cong., 1st sess., 373-77.

16 Jonathan Roberts to Matthew Roberts, Nov. 30, Dec. 8, 1811, Roberts Papers.

port. The House voted on six resolutions submitted by the committee and the Pennsylvania delegation never provided less than fourteen affirmative votes. On five of the rollcalls they voted unanimously in favor of the resolutions. By December 19, all the resolutions had been passed by large majorities. Some hoped that effective preparations for war would force Britain to relent. However, this does not justify the accusation that they were bluffing. Hoping to prevent war by preparing for it, they were quite willing to fight if Britain did not relent. In a speech made later in the session Smilie stated explicitly that he had supported preparedness legislation in the hope that the men and arms provided for would not be used, but he "would now go to war." Manuel Eyre wrote Congressman Findley that he, like Findley, hoped that preparation would avert war, but was prepared to fight if Britain did not relent. Even Roberts stated that he "would be exceedingly glad to remain at peace. The Federalists seem sanguine the orders-in-council will be revoked—I confess I hardly allow myself to hope it."[17]

Reporting public opinion in Franklintown, Pennsylvania, Richard Leech told Roberts that his feelings were in accordance with the report of the Foreign Affairs Committee and that he thought most of his fellow citizens favored it also. The war seemed "just and necessary for the preservation of everything dear to free men." Duane was delighted with the report. Finally the legislature had proposed forceful measures "to defend the rights and honor of the nation" and to impress "those skeptics who doubted the ability of a republican government to function in period of adversity." The state legislature passed resolutions approving the recommendation of the Foreign Affairs Committee and pledging to give full support to

[17] *Annals of Congress,* 12th Cong., 1st sess., 1592; Manual Eyre to William Findley, Jan. 12, 1812, Gallatin Papers; Jonathan Roberts to Matthew Roberts, Jan. 25, 1812, Roberts Papers.

military preparations of the national government and complete support if Congress declared war.[18]

However, submission and approval of the report did not implement it. The effort to enact its proposals into law produced a heated and prolonged debate. From November 1811 until April 1812, Pennsylvania congressmen and their constituents alternated between exhortation and frustration. William Findley was the first Pennsylvanian to speak to the committee's recommendations. On December 24, 1811, he spoke in support of the resolutions authorizing increases in the militia. "The aggressions and bad faith of the British government and the recommendations of the President," he said, "were the foundations of the resolutions before the House. . . . If it is an advantage to a nation to have justifiable cause for war, the United States have possessed that advantage" for many years. "Consulting what we have thought expedient we have borne a testimony against these injuries by every practical restriction short of hostility." Since all peaceful efforts had come to naught, it was time to resort to more energetic modes of resistance. On January 10, 1812, Findley again asserted that war or submission were the only remaining alternatives. The latter was impossible. "I want to engage in war . . . in such a manner as we can support it with honor."

William Crawford, a representative from Adams County just east of the Appalachians, also concluded that there was no alternative to war. Further submission would destroy the Republican party and besmirch the image of republican government everywhere. But, he wrote to Madison, "even among those who have *only* the same objects in view, so much diversity of sentiment prevails; that some means to unite their views and their efforts

[18] Leech to Roberts, Dec. 27, 1811, Roberts Papers; Philadelphia *Aurora*, Dec. 17, 1811; *Pennsylvania Senate Journal*, 1811-1812, pp. 9-12; *Pennsylvania House Journal*, 1811-1812, pp. 104-10.

appears essential to the immediate preservation of the government."[19]

Jonathan Roberts took the same position on the floor of the House as he had taken in his letters to his brother. Preparation for war, he said early in the debate, was a policy "on which we have no choice but to act" because circumstances are such that there is "no alternative but vigorous preparation for resistance, or . . . unconditional submission." Two months later he made the same point. The Republican administrators had "with long continued and unceasing efforts . . . sought to avoid war." Britain's intransigence had left submission to a doctrine of absolute recolonization as the only alternative to war.[20] While the other Republican members of the Pennsylvania delegation did not make any significant speeches during the debate, their votes indicate that they favored war preparations.

The diversity of sentiment of which Crawford spoke prevented Congress from enacting the proposals of the Foreign Affairs Committee into law. During the long winter of debate, it sometimes seemed as if the obstruction of the Federalists, the open opposition of Randolph and his allies, and the quibbling of the moderates would retard preparations, dampen the ardor of the people, and ultimately stop the move toward war. Clay's adroit leadership prodded Congress on, and preparatory measures slowly were passed. Ultimate success was foreshadowed by passage of the Additional Army bill. President Madison had requested an addition of ten thousand men to the regular army. In the Senate antiadministration forces led by Giles raised the figure to twenty-five thousand in an effort to embarrass the administration. This large increase aroused opposition in the House where

[19] Crawford to Madison, March 28, 1812, quoted in Roger H. Brown, *The Republic in Peril: 1812* (New York, 1964).

[20] *Annals of Congress*, 12th Cong., 1st sess., 502-505, 903. See also Roberts' letter to P. Hollingsworth, April 11, 1812, Roberts Papers.

it was argued that such a large force was too expensive and a potential danger to civil liberties. When a compromise was offered providing that officers would not be commissioned or paid until the troops they were to command had been recruited, the moderates accepted, and the bill passed, 90-35. Pennsylvania voted 14-2-2 with Rodman and Smilie opposing and Milnor and Whitehill not voting.[21] The Senate rejected the House compromise, and the House receded from its amendments and accepted the Senate version.[22]

The debate on the Additional Army bill set the style for all subsequent debates on preparedness legislation. As each bill was introduced it faced Federalist obstruction, the opposition of antiadministration Republicans, and was often stalled by regular Republicans who urged caution, raised constitutional questions, or showed great concern over expense. Debate was followed by compromise, and additional measures became law. To those who were committed to war the pace seemed very slow. Pennsylvania Republicans urged their congressmen to act quickly and decisively.[23]

Complaining bitterly about Congress's hesitation, Fox begged Roberts to unite the party. "We [Republicans] cannot all think alike, but a party must act by a system,

[21] *Annals of Congress,* 12th Cong., 1st sess., 617.

[22] *Annals of Congress,* 12th Cong., 1st sess., 718.

[23] The only available correspondence is that of Jonathan Roberts. There is much evidence to suggest, however, that the correspondence he received circulated among other members of the delegation, especially Lacock, Smilie, and Robert Brown. See Jonathan Roberts to Matthew Roberts, Nov. 9, 1811, in which Roberts expressed great satisfaction at having Lacock as a roommate. He states that they exchanged information. In the same letter he expressed "sincere respect" for Smilie. "I feel more inclination to be confidential with him." On May 23, he stated specifically that he had circulated a letter among members of the delegation. Smilie, Findley, and Crawford lived together and certainly exchanged information. Findley to Eyre, Feb. 4, 1812, Gallatin Papers. For the position of antiadministration Republicans, see Norman K. Risjord, *The Old Republicans* (New York, 1965), particularly chapter five.

or it must give way to that which will. It is folly to be
splitting hair at a time like the present. We want 'the
long push, the strong push, and the pull altogether,' of
the whole Republican phalanx."[24] Congress need not fear
that the people will not support a war. "Let the Republicans there act their parts well—the people always sound
at heart will go hand in hand."[25] This from a man who
wrote a month later, "I find my wishes lead still toward
peace. And those wishes are stronger as the time approaches in which I fear a war must come." The war must
come because there was "no mode in which the government can preserve the peace of the country and support
its honor," and because of the "open attack and probable
success of the Federalists" if past policies were continued.[26]

This is a point made by many other correspondents.
Believing that the United States had ample justification
for war, that continuation of the policy of commercial
coercion could only lead to further insults and loss of
honor, many Republicans feared that if effective measures
to protect American rights were not taken soon, the people
would abandon the party and seek other leadership.

Roger Brown contends that one of the impulses to war
was the desire to show that a republican form of government could maintain itself in time of peril. Evidence to
support this thesis in Pennsylvania is scanty. There are
some indications in many of the quotations cited above
that there was concern for the reputation of republicanism. During the war one of the arguments occasionally
used to defend continuation of the war after repeal of
the orders-in-council was the necessity to prove that a
republican government could wage a successful war. On
the other hand, it seems probable that concern for the

24 Findley to Eyre, Feb. 4, 1812, Gallatin Papers.
25 Fox to Roberts, Feb. 2, 1812, Roberts Papers.
26 Fox to Roberts, March 10, 1812, Roberts Papers.

electoral welfare of the Republican party was an important consideration in many minds. The calls for party unity, the many warnings that failure to act would result in losses in the next election, undoubtedly influenced many members of Pennsylvania's delegation and contributed to the remarkable unity of the state's congressmen.

Commenting that the passage of the April embargo had ended all speculation "as to war or no war," Roberts's most regular correspondent stated that "how the Republican party will be upon the final question is a subject of great solicitude. . . . The New York election begins on Tuesday next: the result will be of prime importance." If the Federalists made significant gains, the government would have to exert itself to regain the confidence of the people.[27] John Binns, the editor of the *Democratic Press* in Philadelphia, excoriated the Federalists who had led the opposition to a bill authorizing a government loan. In Philadelphia they had used "the basest schemes, . . . misrepresentations, the vilest artifices" to oppose the loan. They are a "cursed band of factious aristocrats" whose "conduct ought to invigorate every heart that loves our principles and our country." He concluded, "I tell you sir a war is necessary to purge the country of this foul and wicked stuff." Referring to the forthcoming presidential election, he asserted, "if we declare war soon, we shall have all the electoral votes." He made the same point two days later. "A declaration of war is indispensable to preserve our government. The honor of the nation and of the party are bound up together, and both will be sacrificed if war be not declared." Nothing but a declaration of war would "disarm" the Federalists and "invigorate our friends." If war is not declared soon, "evil must follow. If it be done good invaluable must result."[28]

27 Fox to Roberts, April 25, 1812, Roberts Papers.
28 Binns to Roberts, May 3, May 5, 1812, Roberts Papers.

The *Aurora,* in whose columns Duane generally opposed Binns on state issues, held the same views. Federalist opposition to administration measures was ample evidence, Duane argued, that there is a British faction in the United States. In time of war their patriotism would overcome their selfishness, or they would be crushed. On the other hand, if the United States "continue the present course, the people will lose confidence in their government and pride in their nation." Their apathy and lethargy will allow the British party to come to power. "Such an event will spell not only the end of our independence, but the end of our freedom as a people." In the same vein Eyre suggested to Roberts that "moderate Federalists who are men of fortune and character . . . and are willing to offer their services," be given positions in the army. Their efforts should be accepted, he wrote, because such positions would "wean them from their party and would ultimately promote the welfare of the republican government." Federalist opposition to bills to strengthen and prepare the militia for hostilities, Duane contended a few months later, was not based on financial reasons, as their leaders claimed. Distrustful and fearful of the people, Federalists will oppose any measure that will give the people power—military or political. They fear that the public armed with the ballot or gun will prevent them from taking power. Since their only hope for gaining power rests on Britain's ability to destroy our republican institutions they opposed any measure which will enable the people to defend their country. The United States must go to war if for no other reason than to break the British faction and assure the continuation of republican rule.[29]

Federalist attacks on the administration and the hesita-

[29] Philadelphia *Aurora,* Jan. 6, March 12, 1812; Eyre to Roberts, April 19, 1812, Roberts Papers.

tion of Congress have "a tendency to weaken the energies of the party," Thomas Rogers told Roberts. "Let us therefore go to war. A war will prevent all clamors except from tories and we will know how to dispose of them. For my part I think war the only honorable course for Congress to pursue." When war was not declared by the end of May, Rogers told Roberts that a Republican meeting "declared their conviction of the necessity of it. . . . My opinion is the sooner the better, for you may rely on it the people are becoming tired of the suspence [*sic*] they have been in for some time."[30] Another local Republican, John Connelly, demanded vigorous action to prove "to domestic and foreign enemies that Republicans are fully competent to direct the helm of state in peace or war." If war were declared before the summer he "would have no doubt of Madison's election. . . . Decisive measures has [*sic*] now become necessary."[31] A man who claimed to be "a simple constituent" believed he was "expressing the feelings of the great majority" when he remarked that lately "Federalists . . . speak with more confidence against the government but this cannot be more than temporary." Vigorous action on the part of the government would quickly reverse the Federalist onslaught.[32]

On May 20 a meeting of Norristown Republicans sent Roberts and Brown a set of resolutions expressing confidence in the administration and demanding vigorous action. Federalist strength, the resolutions warned, was growing rapidly in the district, and if some action were not taken soon "their future success would be assured." Roberts circulated the petition among the members of the Pennsylvania delegation. "Many pleasantries were indulged in. . . . The voice of 12,000 citizens will have its

30 Rogers to Roberts, May 16, June 1, 1812, Roberts Papers.
31 Connelly to Roberts, May 21, May 26, 1812, Roberts Papers.
32 William Slade to Roberts, May 11, 1812, Roberts Papers.

weight."[33] In June, Fox asked Roberts for a retort to Federalist taunts. Commenting on the Senate's lengthy closed session, he warned Roberts that "people will lose confidence in the government and the system if Congress does not act soon."[34] Another correspondent informed Roberts that "the Republican party highly approve the determined stand of Congress, but many are surprised at the tardiness." He asked whether new blood might not produce more haste and suggested a change in leadership. "If Republicans do not produce bold men and bold measures" the people might easily succumb "to the blandishments of the Federalists."[35]

Just before the declaration of war Richard Leech wrote a long, doleful letter which epitomized the feelings of many Republicans.

> It is impossible for me to describe my present feelings and apprehensions—for about a week past I have been in daily expectation that the deed of deeds was done —the war machine put into active motion. This deed and this alone can save the character of the democratic party and of the nation. . . . Though the House of Representatives has covered itself with glory, I am told the Senate has or will put this country to open shame. . . . Is it possible that a government can have the respect and confidence of its own citizens [if it does nothing] more than talk about its independence and its rights.[36]

These urgings reenforced the predispositions of the state's congressmen. None of them took an active part in the debate, but they all supported the preparedness

[33] Jonathan Roberts to Matthew Roberts, May 23, 1812, Roberts Papers.
[34] Fox to Roberts, June 16, 1812, Roberts Papers.
[35] Isaac Anderson to J. Roberts, May 13, 1812, Roberts Papers.
[36] Leech to Roberts, undated, but obviously written after June 12 and before the declaration of war. Roberts Papers.

measures as they came before the House. On January 10, the day after it passed the Additional Army bill, the House began to consider the bill for raising fifty thousand volunteers. Republican moderates as well as outright opponents raised the serious question of whether the president could, without specific constitutional authorization, order the militia beyond the borders of the United States. For almost a month the House debated subtle constitutional points. After debating numerous amendments, defeating attempts at delay, and presenting counter-proposals, the bill passed without mention of the president's authority. Pennsylvania voted 14-0-4.[37]

Bills relating to the navy were not as successful. Without much opposition the House passed a bill for outfitting existing ships, but traditional Republican antipathy to a large navy caused the defeat of a bill to add twelve ships of the line and twenty frigates to the navy. The most common arguments were that the addition was too expensive and that even with more ships, the fleet would be inadequate to contend with Britain's navy. By a close vote of 62 to 59 the bill failed on January 27. All the Pennsylvania Republicans voted for the measure. Defeat of the naval addition was only a minor setback. Other preparations continued. Ordnance bills, provisions for coastal defenses, and some reorganization of the war department were slowly hammered out and passed by the House. Pennsylvania congressmen supported all of these measures overwhelmingly. Yet a majority for war was still uncertain. Hope of favorable news from England and determined opposition to Gallatin's program for financing the war prevented the final step from being taken.

Gallatin proposed to finance the war by loans, a doubling of the import duties, and, in violation of sacred

37 *Annals of Congress*, 12th Cong., 1st sess., 800.

Republican principle, direct taxes and excise taxes. Each of these measures was debated at length. Direct taxes had a particularly rough going since many congressmen who would vote for taxes opposed any tax that weighed heavily on their own constituents. After much urging and some compromise the financial program finally passed. On February 25 a bill calling for an $11 million loan passed 92-29, with Pennsylvania congressmen dividing 15-3. On March 4, the House approved resolutions imposing direct taxes to be enacted into law when war was declared. The Pennsylvania delegation divided, 12 in favor, 1 opposed, 3 abstaining.[38] None of the Pennsylvania congressmen took an active part in the debate, but by their votes they revealed their commitment to preparation for war, to war itself, and to party regularity. Legislative initiative was not enough. The next step had to come from the president.

On April 1, 1812, in an enigmatic one-sentence message, President Madison recommended to a closed session of Congress the immediate enactment of a general embargo.[39] There has been some controversy concerning the president's motives in recommending the measure and the purposes it was to serve.[40] Ardent supporters of the measure declared it to be a step toward war. Its purpose, supposedly, was to allow American vessels to return safely to port before war was declared. Others saw it as another effort at economic coercion and were not convinced that it would be followed by war. Still others saw the embargo as a final threat. If Britain could be convinced that this

[38] Excellent summaries of the preparedness legislation can be found in Harry L. Coles, *The War of 1812* (Chicago, 1965), 16-26, and Mayo, *Henry Clay, Spokesman of the New West*, 385-465.

[39] *Annals of Congress*, 12th Cong., 1st sess., 1587.

[40] See Perkins, *Prologue*, 384-89; Irving Brant, *James Madison: The President* (Indianapolis, 1956), 424-32; Brown, *The Republic in Peril: 1812*, pp. 99, 103.

embargo was to be the last American effort short of war, she might change her policy.[41]

The congressional debate gives some credence to all of these views. The majority of the Pennsylvania delegation, the Republican press, and leading politicians within the state accepted the embargo as America's last effort short of war. In the first hours of the debate Adam Seybert stated that he felt pledged to go to war and that he was in favor of an embargo as a precautionary measure and precursor to war. Smilie followed immediately, telling the House that the embargo was intended as a war measure. At the beginning of the session he said he "was not so warm for war . . . but . . . would now go to war—if we now recede we shall be a reproach among all nations."[42] Fourteen separate rollcall votes were taken in the House on the bill laying an embargo. In the Pennsylvania delegation fourteen were in favor of the embargo; these voted against any effort to postpone consideration of the measure and against any proposal that would agree to the laying of an embargo, but postpone its application. Two members, the Federalist James Milnor and William Rodman, were opposed to the embargo and when they voted they approved of all efforts at delay and voted against the measure. Whitehill, who in the previous two sessions had always sided with the majority in his delegation, cast one dissenting vote favoring postponement of debate on the embargo bill for one day. William Piper, a new member on the delegation, supported every effort at delay, but voted for the bill.

A bill laying an embargo for sixty days passed the House by a vote of 70-41 on the day the president

[41] The House debate on the April embargo is in the *Annals of Congress*, 12th Cong., 1st sess., 1587-98, 1601-15. The senate debate is in the same volume, 187-94.

[42] *Annals of Congress*, 12th Cong., 1st sess., 1592.

requested it. The Pennsylvania delegation supported the bill 16-2, the same vote by which it supported the war later. The Senate made a series of amendments to the bill, the most important of which extended the embargo to ninety days. To prevent a stalemate between the House and the Senate such as that which had so seriously crippled Macon's proposals in the previous Congress, House Republicans concurred with the Senate amendments by large majorities. Federalist delaying tactics caused eleven rollcall votes to be taken. The lines in Pennsylvania had been drawn on the original measures. Sixteen voted with the majority on every issue (in one rollcall Whitehill's vote is not recorded), while Milnor and Rodman voted with the minority.

In Pennsylvania, Republicans applauded the embargo and viewed it, as their representatives had, as a prelude to war. On April 4, the editor of the *Aurora* speculated on what action Congress might be taking behind closed doors. If war were being proposed, Duane suggested that Congress consider the advisability of a preliminary embargo. Two days later the *Aurora* reported approvingly the passage of the embargo, calling it "the harbinger of a manly contest for essential rights perseveringly trampled upon by the British government." Duane hoped that Congress, having learned from past mistakes, had made adequate provisions for enforcement because even at the brink of war there were still those who placed "personal profit above the honor and independence of their country." The navy, he suggested, should be used to enforce the law: "If it cannot be used to command the respect of foreign nations it may be used to command the respect of our own citizens."[43]

The Carlisle *Gazette* argued that the embargo just passed was not war, and did not inevitably lead to war,

[43] Philadelphia *Aurora*, April 6, April 7, 1812.

but would have to end in war or in an honorable adjustment with the belligerents. The advantages of the embargo as pointed out by the editorial were that it protected men and property already in port; it warned ships at sea to return home for safety; and it informed foreign powers that the time had arrived for the wrongs they had inflicted on the United States to be redressed. The *Gazette* concluded that if the nation's wrongs were not redressed a failure to go to war after the expiration of the embargo would be dishonorable.[44] The Pittsburgh *Commonwealth* saw "the determination of the country to defend its rights at length expressed in the provisionary measure of an embargo."[45]

The Federalist press took surprisingly little notice of the measure. The Pittsburgh *Gazette* and the Pennsylvania *Gazette* both published the text of the law and in each there are letters predicting a serious decline in farm prices. Both papers criticized the embargo. The Pittsburgh *Gazette* called the bill a substitute for action taken by a "timid administration too weak to act and too embarrassed to retreat." The Pennsylvania *Gazette* simply argued that like its predecessor, this embargo would not achieve its intended results and would be harmful to the United States alone.[46]

Correspondents of Jonathan Roberts all approved the measure. John Connelly said the embargo had "for its object and end the honor, dignity and independence of our country." Edward Fox informed Roberts that the embargo, and the war he assumed would follow, would be highly beneficial. It would establish a national character, protect the nation's commerce, increase its manufactures, and wean the country from European particu-

44 Carlisle *Gazette*, April 17, 1812.
45 Pittsburgh *Commonwealth*, April 14, 1812.
46 Pittsburgh *Gazette*, May 1, 1812; Pennsylvania *Gazette*, April 15, 1812.

larity. Edward Stiles told Roberts that "it is the general wish and sentiment in the democratic ranks that Congress will now go on and not attempt to trace back those steps they have taken . . . to have their insulted country's rights respected." Manuel Eyre felt war should be declared before the embargo expired, otherwise "the people will not believe in war." Jones believed that the embargo and subsequent war would develop internal resources and manufactures, and put the United States in a better bargaining position in the future.[47]

An exchange of letters between Congressman Roberts and an Easton miller, Paschal Hollingsworth, provides an interesting summary of the development of Republican thinking. Hollingsworth had written to Roberts and Congressman Robert Brown condemning the April embargo as "highly detrimental" and saying that "inevitable ruin results." In answering the letter Roberts admitted that the embargo and war would cause some private embarrassments. He argued, however, that failure to resort to war without a previous embargo "would work greater evil." In justifying the war, to which the embargo was but a prelude, Roberts cataloged American grievances: impressment, the seizing of American vessels in American waters, the interdiction of commercial intercourse, attempted subversion, negotiation in bad faith. In every instance this nation had attempted negotiation or methods of peaceful coercion—to no avail. "We have no choice but open war or submission to a doctrine of absolute recolonization." If the embargo caused undue hardships on the millers of Easton it is because "they have become victims of a delusion" produced by the minority in Congress that this nation would not protect its interests.

[47] Connelly to Roberts, April 25, 1812, Fox to Roberts, May 4, 1812, Edward Stiles to Roberts, May 30, 1812, Manuel Eyre to Roberts, May 2, 1812, William Jones to Roberts, May 27, 1812, Roberts Papers.

Roberts concluded by telling Hollingsworth that "we owe very much, if not entirely, our necessity to go to war to you and those who think like you. . . . A belief on the part of Great Britain that she has many partisans in America who are able to divide and paralyze our councils . . . has invited and encouraged her aggressions."[48]

Pennsylvania's reaction to the April embargo shows that the people of the state were ready for war. Their congressmen did not disappoint them. The Pennsylvania delegation was the second largest in the House, consisting of eighteen members. Sixteen of them voted regularly with the majority of the House. In many cases the united support of the Pennsylvania delegation was the margin of passage of many measures. The following charts show clearly the united support which Pennsylvania congressmen provided for Republican measures generally and for the war and preparations for war in particular.

These figures indicate a high degree of party regularity. Two recent studies by empirically oriented political scientists who concerned themselves with the problem of party regularity conclude that any legislator who votes with the majority of his colleagues between 63 and 71 percent of the time can be considered a party regular.[49] The sixteen Pennsylvania representatives who voted for

48 Both Hollingsworth's and Roberts's letters are printed in the Philadelphia *Aurora*, April 20, 1812. There is a copy of Hollingsworth's letter as well as a draft of Roberts's reply in the Roberts Papers.

49 Donald R. Matthews, *U.S. Senators and Their World* (New York, 1960), 143; Fred I. Greenstein, *The American Party System and the American People* (Englewood Cliffs, N. J., 1963), 79. Matthews arrived at his 63 percent figure by studying the Senate, Greenstein arrived at 71 percent by studying the House. Neither makes the argument explicitly, but there is a strong implication in both works that the percentage in the House is higher because of the larger membership and shorter terms in that body. The large membership requires greater party cohesion if anything is to be accomplished. The shorter terms, and the general fact that representatives are not as well known by their local constituents as senators, makes strong party identification an important asset for representatives at election time.

CHART I—*Votes of Pennsylvania Delegation on All Rollcall Votes, Twelfth Congress, First Session*

Name	Votes with Majority of Congress	Votes with Majority of Delegation	Votes with Minority of Congress	Votes with Minority of Delegation	% with Majority of Congress	% with Majority of Delegation	Not Voting
William Anderson	150	149	37	35	80.21	80.98	12
David Bard	122	132	28	16	81.33	89.19	49
Robert Brown	146	164	39	18	78.92	90.11	14
William Crawford	148	150	43	38	77.49	79.79	8
Roger Davis	144	147	28	22	83.72	86.98	27
William Findley	155	156	28	24	84.70	86.67	16
John Hyneman	142	157	34	16	80.68	90.75	23
Abner Lacock	151	160	39	27	79.47	85.56	9
Joseph Lefever	115	111	32	35	78.23	76.03	52
Aaron Lyle	163	176	36	20	81.91	89.80	0
James Milnor	55	46	74	82	42.63	35.94	70
William Piper	140	151	34	21	80.46	87.79	25
Jonathan Roberts	157	173	38	19	80.51	90.10	4
William Rodman	76	78	87	83	46.62	48.45	36
Adam Seybert	133	142	45	35	74.72	80.23	21
John Smilie	137	151	36	21	79.19	87.79	26
George Smith	143	144	31	27	82.18	84.21	25
Robert Whitehill	125	140	46	29	73.10	82.84	28

war were all well above either figure. Their percentage with the majority would be even higher if one eliminated from the calculation six votes cast with the minority by most of the members when the House voted against moving the United States Military Academy from West Point, New York, to Carlisle, Pennsylvania. All of the Pennsylvania representatives who voted on questions relating to this move voted in favor of it but were always in the minority. These six votes partially explain the higher percentage of unanimity within the delegation. The figures in column 6 indicate great cohesiveness within the delegation. It cannot be asserted that this unanimity was achieved by conscious efforts by the members, or that they were even aware of it. It may be inferred, however, that the people of Pennsylvania elected representatives of like minds who voted together with remarkable regularity, and gave a high degree of support to the Republican majority.

The raw figures from which the above chart was compiled provide another significant index to the delegation's regularity. In the 199 rollcall votes taken in the first session of the Twelfth Congress, a majority of the Pennsylvania delegation voted with the Republican majority 165 times. A majority of the delegation voted with the minority in only 31 instances, while it divided evenly on three occasions. In percentage terms a majority of the Pennsylvania delegation voted with the Republican majority 82.91 percent of the time. Since there are no similar studies of other delegations, comparisons are impossible. From what is generally known of the makeup of the House in this period, however, one could argue that no other delegation was as united, or gave such support to the Republican party.

Although he voted so infrequently that the figures lose much of their meaning, the votes of James Milnor (not to be confused with William Milnor of the Eleventh Congress), the only Federalist on the delegation, provide a good contrast to the regularity of the Republican congressmen. He voted with the majority only 55 times or 42.63 percent, 32 percent less than the lowest ranking Republican, Adam Seybert. Milnor explained early in the session that he would oppose all preparedness legislation because he did not believe it would "deceive Great Britain . . . and enduce [sic] a revocation of the orders" and he was not convinced that the Republicans really intended to go to war.

The behavior of William Rodman is difficult to explain. He was "an early adherent to the Jeffersonian school of politics" and had a sense of party loyalty. In 1804 he had declined renomination to the state senate stating that at the time of his first election "circumstances made it necessary for every Republican to contribute his services in such a way as his fellow citizens might requre; and I did not then hesitate to serve." When a serious split developed in the state Republican party between the followers of McKean and Snyder, Rodman sided with the Snyder faction which was much more friendly and loyal to the national organization. He ran for Congress in 1808 but was defeated by a slate loyal to the McKean faction. He was one of the Republican electors who voted for Madison that year. He was a Quaker, but this does not seem to have been a decisive consideration as he had accepted a commission in the state militia, and had participated actively in the supression of Fries rebellion. The only other known fact is that he was in bad health during most of the session.

Republican leaders in the district could not explain his action. A local party leader, George Harrison, responding to Roberts's request for information about Rodman commented:

I can state explicitly that I do not know that any person or persons may have written to or influenced him in a departure from his colleagues and the majority in Congress in the measures pursued. I cannot even form a probable conjecture, nor do I at present know any person who is likely to possess the information you ask. I have conversed with several of my neighbors who knew him intimately with myself and who entertain the highest opinion of his democracy and strict integrity [who] are at a loss to account for his conduct. . . . I have such an opinion of his integrity that until the contrary appears, shall believe that no improper motive actuated him [*sic*].

Thomas Rogers told Roberts that "his friends in Bucks County are as much dissatisfied with him [Rodman] as we are here." Referring to a set of resolutions sent from his constituents to himself, Brown and Rodman, Roberts said "they pleased General Brown exceedingly," while Rodman "betrayed some emotion, but showed no contrition." When the petition was circulated among other members of the delegation "many pleasantries were indulged in and some severe things said to [Rodman]." None of this, of course, provides an explanation, but it does show some of the reaction to Rodman's erratic behavior. Roger Brown, who made a thorough study of antiwar Republicans "puzzled over Rodman . . . and tried to find something on him but never got enough to venture an analysis." The only available explanation is that made by Charles Henry Jones in *A Memoir of William Rodman.* According to Jones, "Rodman reluctantly felt himself called upon to differ with his party. Long association and community of principle had attached him to its organization, but he had strong conscientious convictions which refused to be controlled by party discipline. . . . He was far from being a full believer in the Quaker doctrine of non-resistance. . . . But there were occasions when his judgment seemed to be influenced by their doctrines. It was not this particular war. . . . It was aggressive warfare in the abstract."⁵⁰

The people's opinion of the actions of their representatives may be inferred from the fact that the three members of the Twelfth Congress who were not reelected to the Thirteenth were Milnor, Rodman, and Joseph Lefever. The last of these had the second lowest percentage of voting with the majority in the Twelfth Congress (78.23) and supported DeWitt Clinton in the presidential election of 1812.

If the votes of the Pennsylvania delegation in every rollcall taken in the House indicate a noteworthy incidence of party regularity, an examination of ten specific rollcall votes on selected issues demonstrates that their support for war was even more regular than their support for Republican measures generally.

In the chart below, the votes marked 1 to 10 are:

1. On a motion by John Randolph of Virginia that "under existing circumstances it is inexpedient to resort to war."⁵¹
2. On passage of the bill authorizing the president to call up fifty thousand volunteers.⁵²
3. On the bill to authorize the president to call out the militia.⁵³

⁵⁰ Milnor to Bradford, Dec. 10, 1811, Bradford Collection. On Rodman's health and Quaker connections see Jonathan Roberts to Matthew Roberts, Nov. 9, Nov. 30, 1811, March 8, 1812, Rogers to Roberts, Dec. 1, 1811; other references are to George Harrison to Roberts, May 21, 1812, Rogers to Roberts, May 10, 1812, Jonathan Roberts to Matthew Roberts, May 23, 1812, Roberts Papers. For Brown's study of antiwar Republicans see *Republic in Peril,* chapter eight, "Antiwar Republicans," 131-57. His comments on Rodman are in a letter to the author of this work, Aug. 22, 1964.
⁵¹ *Annals of Congress,* 12th Cong., 1st sess., 1470.
⁵² Ibid., 1021.
⁵³ Ibid., 547.

4. On the first four resolutions of the Foreign Affairs Committee (this includes four separate rollcall votes).[54]

5. On passage of the war loan bill.[55]

6. On agreeing to the sixth resolution of the Foreign Affairs Committee which would allow merchant ships to arm in their own defense.[56]

7. On the bill to bring the army to authorized strength.[57]

8. Agreement to all tax resolutions.[58]

9. On the April embargo.[59]

10. To postpone indefinitely the question of adjournment.[60]

If support for war preparations can be interpreted as support for war itself, the chart shows that the Pennsylvania delegation as a body and each congressman had an extraordinary record of support. Excluding the votes of Milnor and Rodman, who voted against the declaration of war, no member cast more than two votes against preparatory measures. Seven members supported all ten measures while six cast only one opposition vote. Looking at the figures from a slightly different direction provides yet another index of unanimity. Again excluding Rodman and Milnor, the Pennsylvania delegation supported six of the ten issues unanimously and cast more than two votes in opposition only once.

Issues 11, 12, and 13 are chosen because they particularly reflect party regularity in that they are party matters.

11. On a seat contested by John P. Hungerford and John Taliaferro of Maryland. Hungerford was a

54 Ibid., 419, 545-47.
55 Ibid., 1092.
56 Ibid., 565.
57 Ibid., 617.
58 Ibid., 1155.
59 Ibid., 1598.
60 Ibid., 1341.

CHART II—*Votes of Pennsylvania Delegation on Selected Rollcall Votes, Twelfth Congress, First Session**

Name	1	2	3	4	5	6	7	8	9	10	11	12	13	14
Anderson	W	W	W	W	W	W	W	W	W	W	W	W	W	W
Bard	W		W	W	W	A	A	W	W	W	W	W	W	W
Brown	W	W	W	W	W	A	A		W	W	W	W	W	W
Crawford	W	W	W	W	W	W	A	W	W	W	W	W	W	W
Davis	W	W	W	W	W	W	W	W	W	W	W	W	W	W
Findley	W	W	W	W	W	W	W	W	W	W		W	W	W
Hyneman	W	W	W	W		W	W	W	W	W	W	W	W	W
Lacock	W	W	W	W	W	W	W	W	W	W	W	W	W	W
Lefever	W		W	W	W	W	A		W	W			W	W
Lyle	W	W	W	W	W	W		W	W	W	W	W	W	W
Milnor	A	A	W	W	A	W	W			A				A
Piper	W	W	W	W	W	W	W	W	A	W	W	W	W	W
Roberts	W	W	W	W	W	A	W	W	W	W	W	W	W	W
Rodman	A	A	W	W†	A	A	A	A	W	A		A	A	A
Seybert	W	A	W	W	W				A	W	A	W	W	W
Smilie		W	W	W	W	W	W	W	W	W		W		W
Smith	W	W	W	W	W		W	W	W	W	W	W	W	W
Whitehill	W	W	W	W	W	A		W	W	W	W	W	W	W

W—vote cast with majority; A—against; blank—not voting.

* This chart confirms the findings of Reginald Horsman's article "Who Were the War Hawks?" *Indiana Magazine of History,* LX (June 1964), 121-36. Using a similar method, but analyzing different votes, he also shows a high degree of unanimity in the Pennsylvania delegation.

† On one of the four rollcalls Rodman was absent.

Quid who had supported Monroe in 1808. Taliaferro was a "regular" candidate.[61]

12. To override a presidential veto on a bill reorganizing the judiciary. Again all the voting members voted with the majority to sustain the veto.[62] There is no rollcall on the original bill, but a motion to reconsider passage of the bill the day after it passed indicates that eight of those who voted to sustain the president's veto had voted for the bill.[63]

[61] Ibid., 395.
[62] Ibid., 1278.
[63] Ibid., 1197.

13. A procedural vote to uphold a decision of the
Speaker on an issue not related to the war. The Pennsylvania delegation voted unanimously to do so.[64]

14. The war vote.[65]

This is a remarkable record of regularity in support of
war measures and party issues. The votes indicate that
among members of the Pennsylvania delegation there
was either a habit of party regularity or strong pressures
to be regular. Whatever else might have prompted them
to support the war, both the habit and the pressure of
party loyalty were significant factors.

The action of the state's two senators during the war
debate, and public reaction to it, also indicates a high
degree of concern with party regularity.

The Senate debated the declaration of war passed by
the House for over a week. Senator Michael Leib, of
Pennsylvania, a leader of an antiadministration faction
called the "Invisibles," supported every effort to defeat
the declaration of war, to amend it drastically, and, when
these efforts failed, to postpone it.[66] Senator Andrew
Gregg, a more regular Republican, who had supported
administration preparedness legislation earlier in the session, also supported the antiwar group. Their motives
are not completely clear. Leib was closely associated in
state politics with Duane of the *Aurora*. The two led
a Republican faction which was opposed to Governor
Snyder and both were hostile to Secretary of the Treasury
Gallatin who used his influence to deny Duane and his
faction federal patronage.[67] Leib undoubtedly hoped to
embarrass the administration, thereby paving the way

[64] Ibid., 1466.
[65] Ibid., 2322.
[66] John Pancake, " 'The Invisibles': A Chapter in the Opposition to
President Madison," *Journal of Southern History*, XXI (1955), 17-37;
Dictionary of American Biography, XI, 150.
[67] Higginbotham, *Keystone*, 72-74, 162, 229, 276; Brown, *Republic in
Peril*, 111.

for the nomination of DeWitt Clinton whose election would benefit him in his domestic factional battles.[68] Gregg's opposition was not based on such a clearly political basis. It will be remembered that as congressman in 1806 he had proposed a stringent nonimportation bill only to see a much more lenient measure adopted. He had also supported the embargo and the nonintercourse bill, and had reluctantly voted for Macon's bill No. 2. In 1809, at the beginning of the first session of the Eleventh Congress, he complained to Samuel Stewart of the "great diversity of sentiment in Congress" and concluded that "we will not strike the first blow. The door for an adjustment of our differences by negotiation will be kept open, should our adversaries be disposed to settle them in that way; but if they are determined on war I expect they will be resisted by a spirit becoming such a nation as ours." By the spring of 1811 he had become totally disenchanted with the policy of economic coercion and what he considered lack of vigor in the administration.[69] He opposed a declaration of war in June 1812 because he believed the nation was not prepared, and doubted the administration's willingness or ability to wage war effectively. In a letter published in the *Aurora* he stated, "To declare war now . . . is tantamount to a paper blockade, for we are *totally unprepared* . . . to carry such a declaration into effect." He favored an adjournment of Congress until the fall to allow time for effective preparation.[70]

In the Senate, Leib had begun his delaying tactics in April when he successfully extended the sixty-day embargo approved by the House to ninety days.[71] Thomas

[68] Rogers to Roberts, June 14, 1812, Jonathan Roberts to Matthew Roberts, June 7, 1812, Fox to Roberts, June 24, 1812, Roberts Papers.

[69] Gregg to Jones, April 8, 1811, Jones Papers; Gregg to Samuel Stewart, Dec. 22, 1809, Gregg Collection.

[70] Philadelphia *Aurora,* June 16, 1812.

[71] *Annals of Congress,* 12th Cong., 1st sess., 187-89.

Rogers opposed this maneuver. It was obviously "intended to divert the attention of the government from a declaration of war," he wrote Roberts. "If the embargo had been adopted as the President and the lower House wished, for sixty days, we would now be acting in earnest."[72] During the war debate Leib at first took only a small part, letting Giles and Smith carry the burden of opposition though he always supported them. Gregg, in fact, played a larger role in the first days of the debate. On June 10, two days after a select Senate committee had reported a war bill, Gregg proposed an amendment to substitute letters of marque and naval reprisals for war. These passed by a margin of 17 to 13, Gregg and Leib voting with the majority. On June 12 both senators voted for a resolution made by John Pope, of Kentucky, which would have included France in the declaration. Gregg's resolutions were brought up again in the same day, but this time lost on a tie vote, Gregg and Leib again voting in favor of them. On June 15, Leib and Gregg voted for two measures which would have delayed a declaration for varying lengths of time, but both were defeated by the Senate by the narrow margin of two votes. In a last desperate effort Leib introduced a proposal very similar to Gregg's of June 10. It authorized immediate maritime war against Great Britain and later, at a specified future date, against France if she did not provide unequivocal evidence that the Napoleonic decrees had been repealed. This proposal was defeated by a narrow margin and by a vote of 19 to 13 the Senate passed the war bill reported by the committee to a third reading and it passed the Senate on June 17. Gregg and Leib voted in favor of the war declaration.[73]

[72] Rogers to Roberts, June 1, 1812, Roberts Papers.
[73] The senate debate is in the *Annals of Congress*, 12th Cong., 1st sess., 265-98. There is an excellent summary in Perkins, *Prologue*, 411-14.

In view of their earlier opposition to war, their votes in favor of the declaration of war can only be explained in terms of party considerations. Gregg was described as "a man of strong party predilections . . . [who] invariably manifested a strong sense of national pride."[74] According to Roberts, when the final issue came his party ties led him to support the war. This was not necessarily a simple matter of loyalty, however. Gregg had gubernatorial ambitions and knew that he had to vote for war if he hoped for Republican support for his ambitions.[75] Leib's action is more difficult to assess. Given his constant opposition to the administration, any future political ambitions he might have had could be served only by Madison's defeat. A vote for war would not erase his past actions. He was thoroughly disliked by many of his colleagues. Roberts believed he deserved to be tarred and feathered and "kicked and scuffed by every honest" man. "If he says three words to me I'll take pains to kick him." Lacock and Brown had the same low opinion of him, and many other administration men in the delegation felt the same way. Binns told Roberts that Republicans of Philadelphia were "anxious and angry" with Leib. "Wagers not a few are laid on Leib's vote." Rogers probably came closest to explaining his vote in one terse sentence. Leib, he said, was "compelled by the sentiment of the people to vote for war." Leib had acted similarly before. In 1808 he had reluctantly supported Snyder's candidacy for the governorship of Pennsylvania because "the current of popular sentiment was too strong" to overcome and he "therefore determined to drift with the tide."[76] Leib explained his

[74] *Dictionary of American Biography,* VII, 595-96.

[75] Jonathan Roberts to Matthew Roberts, June 17, 1812, Roberts Papers.

[76] H. M. Jenkins, *Pennsylvania, Colonial and Federal* (Philadelphia, 1903), 187; Michael Leib to Caesar A. Rodney, Aug. 1, 1808, Gratz Collection.

support for Snyder as an effort to heal "a serious schism in the Republican party." Leib himself substantiated Rogers' statement when he explained that he had voted for war "because my constituents . . . would have made a noise if I had not."[77] Although this cannot be called party loyalty, or party regularity, it certainly indicates that considerations of party politics, particularly the need to retain party support, prompted both senators to vote for a war they did not want at a time they did not want it. In Philadelphia Federalists were "so embittered" that a visitor to that city feared "that the first blood that flows may very possibly be shed in civil strife." But Pennsylvania Republicans rejoiced at the news that Congress had declared war. Their immediate reaction and their longrun support for war reflects the same attitudes they had held in the days preceding the declaration. "The news . . . cheered me," wrote Rogers to Roberts. "If it is true the Republic is safe and we must now rally to the standard." The Federalists "are completely humbled and our friends here are extremely pleased with the result." Referring to the fall elections, he opined that "the Federalists will be stopped short." Roberts told his brother, "the declaration of war is a great point gained." Newspapers carried many reports of county meetings and printed their addresses to the public and toasts drunk at Fourth of July celebrations. These varied in length and style, but the theme was always the same. Independence, which had been declared in 1776, had been threatened by British violations of America's neutral rights. The heroes of 1776, now at the helm of government, were exhibiting the same spirit in defending the independence they had helped achieve. Summarizing the causes of the war, these addresses stress

---

[77] Jonathan Roberts to Matthew Roberts, June 12, June 17, 1812, Binns to Roberts, June 19, 1812, Rogers to Roberts, June 21, 1812, Roberts Papers; Higginbotham, *Keystone*, 255.

maritime grievances and mention Britain's efforts to create internal dissension and her stated ambition to reduce the United States to colonial status. They conclude by asserting that war was just and necessary to protect the nation's rights and to redeem its honor, and by pledging support to the president, the government and republican institutions. Two toasts were particularly common. *"Manufactures*—let us teach the British we can do without theirs, by manufacturing for ourselves" and *"The Pennsylvania delegation* in the legislature of the United States who stood at their posts and declared the existence of a war— May we do our duty as well as they have done theirs."[78]

Governor Snyder's first message after the declaration of war is a good summary of Pennsylvania's reaction. In it he said that the accumulated wrongs and repeated injuries inflicted upon the United States by Great Britain had compelled Congress to declare war to maintain the nation's independence. The Pennsylvania legislature, he said, had "for many years, session after session, approved the measures of the general government and declared that they and their constituents would zealously support all its determinations which promised relief. . . . These determinations are now tested." He hoped that the legislature would rejoice with him that "the day of fruitless negotiation and unavailing resolves [had] passed away." He devoted more than half of his message to a "subject . . . important to our real and practical independence . . . home manufactures." He said he did not wish to express hostility to commerce, but "it must be acknowledged that the embarrassments under which the general government

---

[78] F. H. Gilbert to Sarah Hillhouse, June 20, 1812, Alexander-Hillhouse Papers, Southern Historical Collection, University of North Carolina (Chapel Hill, North Carolina). Rogers to Roberts, June 21, 1812, Roberts Papers. One can find addresses and toasts like those described in virtually any issue of any Republican newspaper. The toasts quoted are from the Washington *Reporter*, July 27, 1812.

has for many years labored has principally, if not exclusively originated in circumstances connected with commerce." The present war provided "a favorable opportunity . . . to foster and encourage the establishment of our own manufactures . . . which secure the real independence of our country."[79] In a set of forthright resolutions the Pennsylvania legislature expressed similar sentiments in approving the war resolution. "After the injustice of Great Britain had by long continued practice acquired the name of right; after the forbearance and negotiating policy had assumed the appearance and acquired the name of cowardice—War is reluctantly, unavoidably, but decisively declared," the legislators stated in the preamble to the resolutions which stated:

> 1. That the declaration of war against . . . Great Britain . . . is the result of solemn deliberations, sound wisdom and imperious necessity.
> 2. That the sword being drawn would never be sheathed till our wrongs are redressed. . . .
> 3. That we pledge our complete support to whatever measures the wisdom of the national legislature may adopt.
> 6. That the promptness, zeal and wisdom with which the governor . . . executed the military orders of the President . . . entitle him to the gratitude of this General Assembly, and of the nation.[80]

The immediate reaction of the people of Pennsylvania to the declaration of war contains all the themes which had prompted them to desire war: concern for the national honor and the nation's independence; the belief that the United States' reliance on Britain for manufactured goods somehow limited the nation's independence and that the

[79] *Pennsylvania House Journal,* 1812-1813, pp. 16-26.
[80] *Pennsylvania Senate Journal,* 1812-1813, pp. 29-31.

road to complete independence lay in the development of domestic manufactures; the concern for the welfare of republican institutions and of the Republican party. These same attitudes sustained the people of Pennsylvania during the two and a half years of the war to which they gave their complete support.

CHAPTER SIX

Pennsylvania at War

During the war Pennsylvania Republicans gave their support to the efforts of the national government. They insisted that the war must be fought to a military conclusion; they cooperated as fully as possible with the national government's efforts to enlist men; and they contributed generously to the financial support of the war. In justifying continuation of the war after news of the repeal of the orders-in-council and military defeats prompted a demand for an immediate negotiated settlement, Pennsylvanians expressed attitudes quite similar to those which had led them to support the declaration of war.

The British Parliament repealed the orders-in-council five days after Congress declared war, but news of the repeal did not reach the United States until late July. Immediately there were demands for a cessation of hostilities and for negotiations to end the war.[1] Republicans believed that repeal of the orders did not eliminate the causes for war. The press interpreted the repeal as a trick to turn the United States away from war and began to insist that Great Britain must satisfy this country on all outstanding issues. William Duane told his readers that the "vague terms in which the repealing order was couched" and the reservation by the Prince Regent of his " 'right' to revive the orders when he might think fit" were sufficient grounds for rejection of the offer. There were still other causes for war which repeal of the orders did not satisfy: the system of paper blockades, impressment of American seamen, the security of the American flag, and the rights of neutral commerce. "The war will be prosecuted, till it produces a peace grounded upon the removal of all the causes of difference and full satisfaction of the injuries hitherto suffered."

Jonathan Roberts told his brother that repeal of the orders was not satisfactory evidence of any basic change in British policy. Like Duane, he referred to the conditional nature of the repeal order and insisted that Britain would have to satisfy the United States on other issues, particularly impressment. John Connelly, Fox, John Binns, and other correspondents made the same point in their letters to Roberts. Rush wrote Ingersoll that he was happy that the United States "took up arms in a just cause," and said, "I am for going on like men notwithstanding old England or new England and if we do fall before both or either to fall at least like resolute men doing their duty." The war, he continued, provided Republicans with a magnificent opportunity. The disaffected must support the war "or put themselves in open opposition." In either case "the cause is strengthened." A Republican meeting in Pittsburgh resolved "that they approve of the manly and dignified ground which the government of the United States has assumed in manifesting its determination to maintain those rights by the sword, a just respect for which it has failed to procure by negociacion [*sic*]." The meeting went on to condemn attempts to sow discord among the people and the demands for peace "when only one cause has been satisfied." The resolutions concluded by urging the people to support Madison and Gerry and

¹ Pittsburgh *Gazette,* Aug. 12, 1812; Pennsylvania *Gazette,* Aug. 14, 1812.

condemning those who would destroy the confidence of the people in their government to gain personal power, office or fortune.[2]

Another reason given for continuing the war in spite of repeal of the orders-in-council was suggested by Roger Brown as a cause of the war—the necessity to establish the ability of a republican government to wage war successfully and, incidentally, of the Republican party to manage a war. Although there is not enough evidence to build a thesis around this point, such sentiments were expressed often enough to suggest that these considerations played a role in determining Republican attitudes toward the war. Arguing against an end to the war in July 1812, Duane implored the people to support the government, urged young men to enlist, and encouraged militia units to volunteer for federal service because a military victory would prove to the world the vitality of Republican government. Jonathan Roberts told his brother that any end of the war before American arms had proved themselves in battle would be "a precursor to the overthrow of the republic and its government." After the early defeats sustained by American forces in the fall of 1812, Republican leaders informed Roberts that even on favorable terms a peace before some military victories would discredit the nation in the eyes of the world, and the administration in the eyes of the people. Binns warned Roberts not to succumb to any offers of peace before the end of the year. There would be congressional elections in the fall and the presidential election to consider. Even serious negotiation with Britain, he warned, would ruin

2 Philadelphia *Aurora*, Aug. 20, 1812; Jonathan Roberts to Matthew Roberts, Nov. 14, 1812, Connelly to Roberts, Oct. 17, 1812, Bills to Roberts, Oct. 23, Nov. 11, 1812, Roberts Papers; Rush to Ingersoll, Oct. 22, Nov. 17, 1812, Ingersoll Papers. For the expression of similar attitudes see Pittsburgh *Commonwealth*, Aug. 29, Sept. 5, Sept. 12, 1812; Pittsburgh *Mercury*, Aug. 25, Sept. 1, Sept. 24, 1812; Washington Reporter, Aug. 28, Sept. 4, 1812; Carlisle *Gazette*, Sept. 19, Sept. 26, 1812.

Republican chances in the fall elections and assure "the success of Federalists or their friends." On the other hand, if the president prosecuted the war vigorously the people would support him even in the face of military reversals.[3]

In the first days of its session the Pennsylvania legislature passed resolutions which called on the administration to prosecute the war until Britain satisfied the United States on all outstanding issues, pledged the support of the state to the war, and denounced the refusal of Connecticut and Massachusetts to supply their quota of militia. In April the legislature debated similar resolutions confirming its belief that the war was just, and once again pledged its support.[4] Major Isaac Roach of the Second Regiment of the United States Artillery explained in his journal that he had enlisted because "it had become a jest and a byword in England that this country could not be kicked into war," and he felt it was necessary to show the world not only that the United States would fight, but that it could fight. Captain Stanton Scholes, who served with a militia unit on the Canadian frontier stated that a desire to repudiate the slurs on the nation's honor had prompted him and many of his comrades to volunteer for militia duty.[5] These and similar sentiments continued to be expressed during the entire course of the war.

These attitudes, and Pennsylvania's devout support of

[3] Philadelphia *Aurora*, July 9, July 11, July 12, July 16, July 23, 1812; Rogers to Roberts, Oct. 19, Nov. 2, 1812, Fox to Roberts, Oct. 23, Nov. 4, 1812, Binns to Roberts, Sept. 14, Sept. 24, Oct. 3, Oct. 11, Oct. 19, Nov. 3, 1812, Roberts Papers. See also Gallatin to Madison, Aug. 8, 1812, in *The Writings of Albert Gallatin*, ed. Henry Adams (Philadelphia, 1879), I, 523. Jefferson to Wright, Aug. 8, 1812, in *The Writings of Thomas Jefferson*, ed. A. A. Lipscomb and A. E. Bergh (Washington, D.C., 1903), VIII, 184. For the military history of the war see H. L. Coles, *The War of 1812* (Chicago, 1965).

[4] *Pennsylvania Senate Journal*, 1812-1813, pp. 29-35, 75-79; *Pennsylvania House Journal*, 1812-1813, pp. 29, 89-97.

[5] "Journal of Major Isaac Roach," *Pennsylvania Magazine of History and Biography*, XVII (1893); Diary of Captain Stanton Scholes, Western Pennsylvania Historical Society, Pittsburgh.

the war and of James Madison's administration, were expressed very clearly in the elections of 1812. The most important contest, of course, was between James Madison and DeWitt Clinton for the presidency. Concurrently, Pennsylvania voters had to elect a new congressional delegation, now expanded to twenty-three members, ninety-five members of the state House of Representatives, and nine state senators. The war and its conduct were the central issues in the campaign, and the results were an impressive victory for James Madison and war.

On May 29, 1812, ambitious New York Republicans, long resentful of Virginia's domination of the party, nominated DeWitt Clinton to oppose Madison in the fall elections. There was little hope of winning western or southern support for his candidacy, but Clinton's chances of winning were good if an alliance could be formed between New England Federalists and middle state Republicans. The chances of getting the support of Pennsylvania Republicans were slim. On March 7, Republicans in the Pennsylvania legislature "nobly and independently declared unanimously in favor of the re-election of Mr. Madison." The legislature had pledged the state's twenty electors to Madison, and the state "will decidedly accord in sentiment."[6]

Clintonians made strenuous efforts to win the support of Pennsylvania Republicans, but did not attract anyone of great influence. They did manage to create a vocal, although ineffective, organization devoted to Clinton's candidacy. This body was organized at a secret meeting in Lancaster in August 1812, at which Congressman Joseph Lefever presided. The meeting issued an address to the people of Pennsylvania urging them to support Clinton. It also urged Republicans in favor "of an honorable peace" to hold similar meetings in support of Clinton, and, it

[6] Dorothie Bobbe, *DeWitt Clinton* (New York, 1933), 184-87; Binns to Smilie, March 19, 1812, Gallatin Papers.

appears, launched a journal dedicated to Clinton's election. The Pennsylvania *Farmer*, which began publication in August 1812, carried little advertising and virtually no local news. Its columns were filled with public addresses and letters favorable to Clinton, the resolutions and addresses of county meetings which had supported Clinton, and detailed descriptions of American military defeats. Beginning in September, it printed under its masthead one of these biblical quotations: "The Way of Peace they know not and there is no judgment in their doing" or "Wherefore Brethren look ye out among you men of honest report whom we may appoint over this business." It ceased publication in February 1813.[7]

The public addresses in favor of Clinton, the resolutions of Clintonian county meetings, and the columns of the Federalist press, the Pittsburgh *Gazette*, the Pennsylvania *Gazette*, and the allegedly independent Pennsylvania *Farmer* express the issues on which antiadministration Republicans (and Federalists who supported them) placed their hopes. The most common charges made against Madison were the unconstitutionality and corruptness of nomination by congressional caucus, the Virginia dominance of the Republican party, and the inept conduct of the war. Warnings concerning heavy taxation to pay for the war and charges that Madison declared war at the behest of Napoleon, thereby involving the United States in an alliance with France, were also common.

The resolutions of a meeting of York County Republicans, typical of similar resolutions by pro-Clinton meetings all over the state, contain all of these charges:

> Because he has precepitately [*sic*] and rashly urged
> Congress to declare war at a time when the country

[7] The best report of this meeting and of the probable connection between Clintonians and the Pennsylvania *Farmer* is in the Pittsburgh *Commonwealth*, Sept. 5, 1812.

was unprepared with the means of carrying it to success.

Because the inauspicious circumstances under which the war was commenced and the weakness with which it has thus far been conducted furnish no flattering pre-sage that the same councils will bring it to a speedy and honorable termination.

Because Mr. Madison is devoted to a Southern policy which is hostile to commerce and consequently discouraging to agriculture the two great sources from which Pennsylvania derives her prosperity.

Because Virginia has already had the presidency twenty years out of twenty four—and now claims it again—thus endeavoring by usage to establish a perpetual right to furnish incumbents for that high office.

Therefore this meeting resolves to concur with the Republicans of the state of N. Y. in the nomination of DeWitt Clinton—not more distinguished for his talents and patriotism than for his adherence to republican principles; yet unlike Mr. Madison, he is a friend to peace and commerce.[8]

A meeting in Dauphin County announced that Madison had been nominated by an unconstitutional caucus "polluted by executive influence, official influence and foreign influence." The defeats sustained by American arms proved the inability of the Madison administration to conduct the war successfully. Virginia had had every president but one since the establishment of the nation and it was time to break her monopoly.[9] This charge was buttressed by appeals to state pride. Pennsylvania had not received its fair share of high federal offices and had been neglected in the military appointments following the declaration of war. A correspondent in the Pittsburgh

8 Pittsburgh *Gazette,* Sept. 18, 1812.
9 Pennsylvania *Farmer* (Lancaster), Aug. 26, 1812.

Gazette suggested that perhaps Pennsylvania's support of "Virginian administrations" had been so constant that they were taking it for granted. A vote for Clinton in this election might regain for Pennsylvania a just share of federal offices. Meetings of Clinton Republicans in York, Lancaster, Nazareth, Bucks, and Luzerne counties deprecated the paucity of Pennsylvanians in federal office and nominated Jared Ingersoll, the father of Charles J. Ingersoll of Pennsylvania, a Republican representative in the Thirteenth Congress, to be Clinton's running mate. Probably to exploit this dissatisfaction Clinton accepted him.[10]

Defending Lefever against the charge of being an apostate, the *Farmer* argued that he was an "honorable man" entitled to the thanks of every true American. "He voted for war. He did so under a sincere conviction that it was right. He has not changed his opinion." But "having seen the gross misconduct of Madison and his ministers he has had the honesty publicly to speak of it" and demand an end "to a flimsily disguised *Southern aristocracy* who wish still longer to lord it over their northern brethren."[11]

Inept conduct of the war was another common charge made against Madison, but the very way in which this issue was handled by Clinton's supporters attests to the strong Republican support for the war in Pennsylvania. They denounced the incompetent generals Madison had appointed, hinting darkly that the appointments were political. They commented on the disastrous effects of the war on commerce, suggesting that the destruction of commercial interests was a prime purpose of the war. They censured Madison for forcing a declaration of war before the country was prepared, and demanded that he dismiss the incompetent members of his cabinet who were

---

[10] On the nomination of Ingersoll, see Irving Brant, *James Madison: Commander-in-Chief, 1812-1836* (Indianapolis, 1961), 106. The quotation is from the Pittsburgh *Gazette*, Sept. 4, 1812.

[11] Pennsylvania *Farmer,* Sept. 2, 1812.

blamed, equally with him, for American defeats. Clinton, they promised, "would soon retrieve the loss by wisdom in council and vigor in execution." In its formal endorsement, the Pittsburgh *Gazette* supported Clinton because his election promised "a vigorous prosecution of the war and a determined character in the relations of peace." Clinton's supporters in Pennsylvania attacked the war from many directions but never the war itself, as did his supporters in other areas.[12]

Pennsylvania Republicans took Clinton's challenge seriously, aware that the results would have national importance. The *Aurora*, which on the whole was strangely quiet during the campaign, refused to give Madison a formal endorsement until late October. At issue in the election was the question of "whether the principles of the declaration of independence shall be upheld by the people; whether a war for our republican form of government . . . shall receive the support of the people."[13] Richard Rush told Charles Ingersoll that the election "is a great cause, and if it succeeds gloriously, as I trust it will, will do wonders for our posterity as well as the nation at present. It will break the bones of the monster, British influence." Rush asked Ingersoll to make the Pennsylvania results known as quickly as possible, because a republican majority there would influence the results in other states. "An influential Maryland democrat assured me they (the Pennsylvania results) will have a favorable effect upon the election in Maryland. . . . Mr. Cutts of Massachusetts . . . is afraid we will lose N. H. though thinks we should not if the favorable results of the Pennsylvania election was [*sic*] known beforehand."[14]

---

12 Pennsylvania *Farmer*, Sept. 2, 1812; Pittsburgh *Gazette*, Sept. 11, 1812. For the conduct of Clinton's campaign in other areas see Dorothie Bobbe, *DeWitt Clinton* (New York, 1933), 182-88, 190-96.
13 Philadelphia *Aurora*, Oct. 13, 1812.
14 Rush to Ingersoll, Oct. 1, Oct. 29, 1812, Ingersoll Papers.

Support for Madison in Pennsylvania was overwhelming. Fourteen of the state's delegation to Congress attended the caucus which renominated him in May 1812, and all voted for him. Of the five who were absent, wrote Roberts, "Crawford pleaded sickness and Whitehill professes concurrence. Lefever and Seybert will go along." Of Leib he said, "his heart is with Clinton, but he was forced to attend the caucus and vote for Madison or be set down as a malcontent without the means of mischief. Judge Anderson [Congressman William Anderson of Pennsylvania] tells me he professes a wish to unite with the Clinton faction—on what basis I know not." Gregg, he said, "has become more affable and the Senators and Representatives from Pennsylvania may yet act with concert."[15] Lefever, as has been shown, led the Clintonian organization and Leib openly supported Clinton in the fall. The fact that he voted for Madison's nomination, however, is indicative of the strength of public sentiment, given Leib's demonstrated proclivity for drifting with the tide. Rodman did not attend the caucus and was defeated as a Clinton candidate for Congress. Even before Madison had been nominated by the caucus, Republican members of the state legislature met on March 7, 1812, prepared an electoral ticket, and all pledged their support to him.[16]

During the campaign, Pennsylvania Republicans, with the notable exception of Duane, stoutly defended Madison against the charges made by the Clintonians, worked hard to prevent further divisions in the party, and in the end gave him a large majority on election day. To the charge that nomination by congressional caucus was unconstitutional, they countered that the Constitution pre-

[15] Jonathan Roberts to Matthew Roberts, May 20, 1812, Roberts Papers; Niles *Register*, II (May 23, 1812), contains the entire proceedings of the caucus.

[16] Philadelphia *Aurora*, March 28, 1812; Pittsburgh *Commonwealth*, April 7, 1812; Charles H. Jones, *A Memoir of William Rodman* (n.p., 1867), 37.

scribes no method for nomination, therefore no method could be constitutional or unconstitutional. If the objection to congressional nomination is the undue influence of a particular group or section, Pennsylvania Republicans replied that nominations made by the legislature of one state are "equally worthy of condemnation. The members of Congress, representing all states and parts of the Union, are certainly better qualified to express the wishes of the nation; being thoroughly acquainted with the nation's problems, they are better qualified than a state legislature to assess its needs."[17]

Answering a letter sent him by a correspondence committee of Adams County which urged him to support Clinton, Congressman Crawford denied the validity of the committee's constitutional objections to the method of Madison's nomination on the same grounds as had the *Mercury*. If nomination by congressional caucus is unconstitutional, he asked, how can nomination by a state legislature be constitutional. If nomination by congressional caucus was objected to because of the alleged undue influence of Virginia, does not nomination by state legislatures present the possibility of collusion among particular states to keep the presidency for themselves. He accused the Clintonians of "the manufacturing of artificial issues" to distract the people and to divide them "during a crisis of such magnitude . . . when the very existence of republicanism itself may be at stake." This consideration alone "will prevent any citizen who wishes to give his support to a continuance of those governing principles from aiding or abetting you in your present scheme." He concluded by urging them to give up their plan and unite behind Madison.[18]

17 Pittsburgh *Mercury*, Sept. 17, 1812.
18 Crawford's letter is printed in the Pittsburgh *Mercury*, Sept. 17, 1812, the Pittsburgh *Commonwealth*, Sept. 19, 1812, and the Washington *Reporter*, Sept. 23, 1812.

To the charge of French influence in the administration, Madison's supporters countered with evidence of Federalist support for Clinton which, in effect, meant British influence in his favor. In a front page article in very large print the Pittsburgh *Commonwealth* announced that a caucus of the Federalist party in New York City had decided not to nominate a candidate of their own, but to support "that candidate of the two already in nomination, whose success would best promote the objects of their party." The caucus had decided to "give preference to Mr. Clinton." The Federalists who attended this meeting were told by one of their members that "Clinton has declared *that all political connection between himself and the Democratic party has ceased and would not again be renewed.*" The *Commonwealth* was so sure of these charges that it concluded the report with the statement: "This fact can be established by a court of law if necessary."[19] In the minds of most Republicans, Federalist support of Clinton was enough to damn him. The connection between the Federalists and the British was assumed to be so well established that it was hardly mentioned. "The condition of the bargain offered by the Federalists and embraced by the Clintonian party were . . . that in the event of the election of their candidate a cession of hostilities against the British should take place within twenty four hours." The *Commonwealth* stated that "in addition Federalists had been promised abundant patronage, had been promised that the capital would be moved to New York or Philadelphia, and that a hereditary Senate would be established."[20]

Clinton's promises to prosecute the war to a victorious conclusion should not be taken seriously, warned the press. "In the west where there is and has been an honorable

[19] Pittsburgh *Commonwealth*, Oct. 27, 1812.
[20] Pittsburgh *Commonwealth*, Oct. 6, 1812.

display of national spirit . . . Mr. Clinton is recommended as a friend of war—he is to carry it on with vigor—in the East he is presented as a friend of peace." One needed only examine the nature of Clinton's support, stated the Carlisle *Gazette,* to know that his promises of vigorous prosecution would not be kept. His supporters were men "who can truly be denominated nothing better than disorderly." Hardly had war begun when they began "to cry for peace, come of our honor and national character what will." The *Commonwealth* stated that Federalist obstruction to peaceful methods of coercion had forced the United States to war and now they opposed it. The defeats of the United States sustained in the summer and fall could not be attributed to incompetence on the part of the administration but they could be attributed easily to Federalist opposition to preparedness legislation and the Federalist obstruction of the war effort. "The present administration is pledged to fight this war to an honorable conclusion" and to "retrieve the lost honor and independence of the nation." Only the election of James Madison would assure "that the war will be fought to a successful conclusion."[21]

Madison's prospects were heightened by the great efforts made by all Republican factions to unite behind Madison and the war effort. John Spayd, the candidate of the anti-Snyder faction in the gubernatorial elections of 1808 is known to have attended unification meetings in Berks and York counties, and in Philadelphia, where he urged unity not only in the presidential election, but also in the congressional elections and in state and local races. In Philadelphia William J. Duane, son of the editor of the *Aurora,* and Alexander J. Dallas, a leader of the anti-

---

21 Pittsburgh *Commonwealth,* Sept. 15, Sept. 22, Oct. 6, Oct. 13, 1812; Pittsburgh *Mercury,* Sept. 17, Sept. 24, Oct. 14, Oct. 22, 1812; Carlisle *Gazette,* Sept. 18, Sept. 25, Oct. 7, Oct. 14, 1812.

Snyder faction, worked hard to unite the city's Republicans. Finally, the *Aurora,* which had called for united support for war, but had maintained a studied silence concerning the election, came out for Madison. On October 13, Duane replied to "some upbraidings and reproaches, and not a little abuse" which he had received "for not taking a more vigorous part in the election" with the statement, "let very well alone." He predicted 145 electoral votes for Madison and a maximum of 73—New York, Delaware, Massachusetts, Maryland (5), and Kentucky (3)—for Clinton. On October 17, he formally endorsed Madison.

Factional politics were confused in Pittsburgh. There was a personal struggle for party control between the editors of the *Commonwealth* and the *Mercury* and between the groups represented by each faction. The groups agreed in supporting Madison and the war, but there was a difference of opinion concerning state and local offices and the congressional candidate. Ultimately they were able to unite behind a unified ticket. This alliance must have been rather shaky, however, because the Federalists, hoping perhaps to capitalize on Clinton's candidacy, but obviously encouraged by the Republican split, offered their own ticket for the first time since 1808. Pittsburgh Federalists confined themselves to attacks on the conduct of the war and never condemned the war itself. This is indicative of the strength of prowar feeling in that area.[22]

These efforts to achieve party unity must have been successful because the election produced an impressive Republican victory. In the state elections on October 13, Republicans won 77 of 95 seats in the Pennsylvania House and 6 of 9 races for the state Senate. In the congressional

---

[22] This discussion is based on an analysis of the Philadelphia *Aurora,* the Pittsburgh *Commonwealth,* and the Pittsburgh *Mercury* for the Republican side and the Pittsburgh *Gazette* and the Pennsylvania *Gazette* for the Federalist side in the late summer and fall of 1812.

elections Republicans won 22 of 23 seats. The lone Federalist to win was John Gloninger whose victory can be attributed in large measure to a Republican split in Dauphin County, which resulted in two candidates being nominated.[23]

In the presidential contest the Republicans won a complete victory, claiming all of Pennsylvania's 25 electoral votes. Madisonian electors won their races by an average margin of 20,000 votes. The importance of these results cannot be overestimated. They assured the administration a large delegation pledged to support its program in the Thirteenth Congress. They assured the national government of the continued cooperation of the state of Pennsylvania and, most importantly, they insured Madison's reelection. He won with a total of 128 electoral votes to 89 for Clinton. Had Pennsylvania voted the other way, Clinton would have won by 11 votes.[24]

The *Aurora* viewed these results as proof that the people of Pennsylvania approved of the war and were determined to fight to maintain "their rights, their freedoms and the independence of their nation." The results also proved that a government "dependent on the people can be sure of their support when circumstances force it to adopt measures which cause temporary misery." The Pittsburgh *Mercury* stated that the election "has terminated in a manner becoming the character of the nation." Richard Rush was elated by the results. The election, he admitted, was "pretty close work, and Pennsylvania as usual, carries the nation on her back." Madison's victory was so impres-

---

[23] Gloninger served for only a few months, resigning in the spring of 1813. He was replaced by Edward Crouch, the candidate of the regular Republicans in the regular election. H. M. Jenkins, *Pennsylvania, Colonial and Federal* (Philadelphia, 1903), 194.

[24] The average for Madisonian electors was 48,946; for Clintonian electors 29,056. For the election results see Philadelphia *Aurora*, Nov. 20, 1812, and Edward Stanwood, *History of the Presidency* (New York, 1892), 104.

sive, he concluded, that "the British faction must be forever quiet." Madison's victory in Pennsylvania can in large measure be attributed to the united Republican support for the war. Having submerged factional differences in order to give united support to measures of economic coercion, having demanded and strongly supported a declaration of war, Pennsylvania Republicans were unwilling to desert the administration which had begun the war which they had demanded. In the words of Henry Adams, "once more the steadiness of Pennsylvania saved the administration."[25]

The state of Pennsylvania expressed its support for the war not only by providing the administration with twenty-two congressmen who would support its measures in Congress, and by providing the commander-in-chief with the margin of victory in his election, but by very sincere efforts to cooperate with the government by contributing men and money to the war effort.

In his opening message to the twenty-third session of the state legislature, Governor Snyder pledged the state's support of the war effort and painted an overly optimistic picture of the military situation. He declared that the nation's frontiers were secure and that the enemy had found it expedient to depart. The privations of the nation had not been "at all proportional to what was expected; much less have we suffered the manifold calamities which the fears of the timid or the treachery of the factious had pourtrayed [sic]." The military reverses suffered in the summer and fall were not due to weakness or incompetence, but to the fact that "for thirty years . . . the attention of the government and of our people [was] solely directed to cultivate the arts of peace." Defeats and

[25] Philadelphia *Aurora*, Oct. 21, 1812; Pittsburgh *Mercury*, Nov. 5, 1812; Washington *Reporter*, Jan. 18, 1813, expresses the same sentiments. Rush to Ingersoll, Nov. 14, 1812, Ingersoll Papers.

reverses should be expected in all wars and the United States should not expect to be exempted. Because the American people have more at stake than any other people on earth, "they will unshakingly and undismayed . . . meet misfortune."[26] This optimism is indicative of Pennsylvania's attitude toward the war.

The legislature responded to the message by passing resolutions praising the governor's patriotism and his prompt compliance with the militia requisitions of the national government during the recess of the General Assembly. The same resolutions applauded the many volunteers who had responded to the governor's request, enabling him to fill the requisition without having to resort to a draft of the militia. It also adopted resolutions appealing for continuation of the war until all outstanding issues were settled and again condemned Massachusetts and Connecticut for their obstructionism.[27] More substantially, it passed a bill authorizing the governor to subscribe one million dollars to the new government loan, ordered the governor to supply Pennsylvania troops serving on the Northwest frontier with adequate clothing, and provided for a bonus of twenty dollars to any volunteers who would serve two months beyond the term of their enlistment.[28]

Throughout the entire war Governor Snyder made every effort to cooperate with the national government in its efforts to organize the state militia into an effective fighting force. Every requisition made of Pennsylvania was met, first by volunteers and later by militia drafts. The

[26] *Pennsylvania House Journal,* 1812-1813, pp. 21-32.
[27] *Pennsylvania Senate Journal,* 1812-1813, pp. 35-49; *Pennsylvania House Journal,* 1812-1813, pp. 89-97.
[28] *Pennsylvania Senate Journal,* 1812-1813, pp. 183, 202, 209-17, 347-49, 643-46; *Pennsylvania House Journal,* 1812-1813, pp. 459, 490-97, 500-502; *Pennsylvania Archives,* 4th series, IV, 828, 9th series, V, 3289-95, 3348-65.

ineffectiveness of the Pennsylvania militia was the result of the confusion in the state's militia laws and the unbelievable lack of coordination between state and national officials. Snyder and his predecessor, McKean, were aware of the confusion of the state's militia laws and every one of their opening messages to the legislature called for sweeping revisions. Every session of the legislature from 1808 to 1814 debated the issue and some minor changes were made, but the state militia was never competently organized.

Failure to provide for the proper arming, disciplining, and staffing of the state militia were, according to the governors, the most serious defects of the state's militia laws. The laws also did not provide for statewide uniformity in the organization of units. These problems might have been overcome had there been some coordination between the state and national governments. All of Snyder's efforts to cooperate proved futile and the fourteen thousand Pennsylvania militia which were ultimately detached to federal service contributed little to the war effort because of the confusion. Three problems, particularly, prevented effective use of the militia.

As soon as Pennsylvania militia were ordered into federal service a question arose as to who was responsible for the paying and equipping of the men. The national government argued that state militia detached to federal service should come fully equipped, and that the government was under no obligation to provide for them until the men arrived at the place to which they had been called and passed to the command of a United States commander. Governor Snyder, on the other hand, held that it was the responsibility of the national government to outfit troops in its service and that the state should be reimbursed for any material which state militia brought with them when they entered national service.

The first state troops called into federal service faced this problem. The government asked Snyder for two thousand troops to rendezvous at Meadville and Pittsburgh and to proceed to Buffalo. The detachment had been filled from those militia companies who had responded to the governor's call of the previous May for volunteers. The officers of these companies informed the governor that because they lacked arms, ammunition, and equipment they were unprepared. The governor responded that he had assumed they were prepared when he had accepted their offer. He told them he had no material at his disposal and suggested that they collect whatever equipment was available—using muskets when rifles were unavailable—and attempt to borrow equipment from companies that had not been ordered up. He then wrote officers of other militia companies in the area asking them to contribute equipment to supply the detachment going to Buffalo. Once the troops arrived at Meadville the problem became more complicated. State law prohibited the governor from paying for supplies in advance, and the national government refused to provide them until the men left the state. The governor suggested to company commanders that they buy supplies on their own account and promised that they would be reimbursed by the state. These problems were not solved during the war and constantly hampered effective use of the militia.[29]

29 James Trimble (deputy secretary of the Commonwealth of Pennsylvania) to Cochran, Sept. 21, 1812, Snyder to Kelso, Sept. 15, 1812, Trimble to Thomas, Sept. 16, 1812, Snyder to Eustis, Sept. 5, 1812, Boileau (secretary of the Commonwealth of Pennsylvania) to deputy quartermaster general of the United States, April 1, 1813, *Pennsylvania Archives*, 2d series, XII, 617, 621, 646, 916. The issue becomes even more clouded if the relations between the state government and its suppliers are considered. There are many letters in the *Pennsylvania Archives* indicating that suppliers requested payment from the state, were directed to the national government, which refused to pay and redirected the collectors to the state. See for example Boileau to Ebenezer Denny, Sept. 5, 1812, April 1, 1813.

A variation to this problem concerned the payment of the men and the disposition of arms that the militia brought with them into federal service. Congress had provided for the distribution of arms to the states according to a prescribed quota. What happened when state militia equipped with arms provided by the national government was called into national service? Snyder believed that "arms removed from the jurisdiction of the state" should be replaced to enable the state to arm new militia units. The secretary of war did not accept this argument and refused to replace the equipment. Governor Snyder let the men and arms go without too much protest, only to find that future requisitions could not be easily met because the state militia was not armed. Every time a detachment of state militia was called into federal service this argument began anew; it was never permanently solved.[30] The problem concerning pay was the same. The state insisted that the national government assume responsibility for payment of the men as soon as they were called, or when they reached the rendezvous. The national government refused to pay until the men joined the regular forces and came under command of a United States commander.[31]

The effectiveness of the Pennsylvania militia was further limited by differences in the command structure between it and the regular forces. In Pennsylvania volunteers were allowed to elect their officers up to the regimental level; officers for drafted militia were appointed by the governor. When volunteer units were combined with drafted units for detachment to national service the problems of command became almost insurmountable.

[30] See Boileau and Snyder to Monroe, *Pennsylvania Archives*, 2d series, 728-37.

[31] Boileau to Samuel Cooper, March 7, 1814, Boileau to Col. James Fenton, May 24, 1814, "To the U. S., therefore, you are to look for your monthly pay," *Pennsylvania Archives*, 2d series, XII, 711-19.

Volunteers claimed they retained the right to elect their officers, even though in service of the national government, and refused to serve under appointed officers. In most instances the problems were solved on an *ad hoc* basis after repeated urgings by the governor, but no permanent solution was ever produced and command problems continued to hamper the effectiveness of the militia. The case of six hundred volunteers sent to assist with the defense of Philadelphia provides a case in point. In offering them Snyder told Monroe that the men had volunteered "under the impression that they would be commanded by officers of their own choosing" and that they "would not readily submit to a consolidation of companies, or any organization that would divest them of their privileges." He wrote to the elected commanders of the unit urging them to cooperate fully with federal officers in Philadelphia.[32] Even if differences over equipment and pay were solved, there remained the problem of integrating the Pennsylvania militia and its officers into the national forces. The command structure of the militia was entirely different from the command structure of the federal service, causing untold difficulties for United States commanders. General Harrison wrote to Snyder almost pleading for changes in Pennsylvania's militia laws to permit effective integration of the state's forces. The major problem was that Pennsylvania militia officers commanded units which were commanded by lower ranking officers in the regular service. When attached to regular army units, Pennsylvania officers refused to accept the lower ranks specified by federal regulations. Finally at Snyder's request, the General Assembly passed a law ordering Pennsylvania officers to "assume the rank to

[32] Snyder to Monroe, *Pennsylvania Archives*, 2d series, XII, 741. See also the correspondence between Raguet, Biddle, and General Bloomfield (United States commander in Philadelphia), 722-25.

which . . . they are entitled" by the laws of the United States, but this did not completely solve the problem.[33]

It is not surprising that the Pennsylvania militia was ineffective. The few letters of John Patterson, a private in the state militia serving on the northern frontier, show the effect of the confusion on the common soldier. Three themes stand out in his letters to his wife. He promised to send money when he was paid and he always said he would be paid soon. He complained of marching and countermarching which made no real progress and intimated that he and the other men believed that the commanders did not know their own minds. Finally, he complained of the lack of provisions and the inadequacy of arms.[34]

That as a fighting force the Pennsylvania militia was ineffective cannot be denied. However, the legislature and the governor attempted to cooperate. Pennsylvania contributed more militia to the federal service than any other state, and at the end of the war collected $188,900 from the federal government for expenses incurred in providing militia.[35]

The state's efforts to cooperate in the financing of the war proved more successful. Secretary of the Treasury Gallatin planned to finance the war by borrowing, without resort to any additional taxation.[36] The state and the

[33] Snyder to Armstrong, April 1, 1813, *Pennsylvania Archives,* 2d series, XII, 619. See also the correspondence between Boileau and General Winder, General Meade, and Secretary Armstrong, *Pennsylvania Archives,* 2d series, XII, 643.

[34] "Letters of John Patterson, 1812-1813," *Western Pennsylvania Historical Magazine,* XXIII (1940), 99-109. Edward J. Wagner discusses all of these problems in great detail in "State and Federal Relations During the War of 1812" (unpublished Ph.D. dissertation, Ohio State University, 1963).

[35] *American State Papers: Military Affairs,* 511.

[36] The financing of the War of 1812 is an extremely complicated subject. It is handled best in Alexander Balinky, *Albert Gallatin, Fiscal Theories and Policies* (New Brunswick, 1958). Also useful are Raymond Walters, *Albert Gallatin* (New York, 1957), and Davis R. Dewey, *Financial History of the United States* (New York, 1920).

citizens of Pennsylvania contributed money generously to all the government loans. The first war loan, offered in May 1812, failed dismally, but the failure cannot be attributed to Pennsylvania. In its twenty-second session the state legislature passed a law authorizing banks in which the state held stock to subscribe to government loans to the value of state-owned stock in the bank. The state pledged to pay interest and principal if the national government defaulted. Under provisions of this law Pennsylvania banks contributed $1,432,800 to the $11 million loan of 1812. Individuals in Philadelphia added another $407,000 bringing the state's total subscription close to $2 million. If other states had contributed proportionately, the loan would have been oversubscribed. Pennsylvania would have subscribed even more if Gallatin could have arranged terms with Stephen Girard.

Girard had recently opened a bank in Philadelphia, and when the loan was announced he agreed to subscribe $1 million. His explanation for making this offer is instructive because it reflects the attitude of the business community generally. Among personal reasons for subscribing to the loan, he believed it to be a good investment. His capital would be placed "at interest with perfect security." He also hoped to gain "the personal consideration which will attach to a citizen being of assistance to the government at this time and to such an extent." Patriotic lending was good business. Although the $1 million was never subscribed by Girard because certain details could not be arranged, his offer indicates confidence in the government and a willingness to support the war.

The loan of 1812 was never fully subscribed. Eyre attributed the failure to the exertion made by the president and trustees of the first Bank of the United States to keep people from subscribing to the loan. "There are a few Federalists here who have acted independently and honorably, and have given encouragement to it." He also believed that the loan had not been fully subscribed because the people were not yet convinced that war would be declared. Had that step been taken "the loan would have been filled without difficulty."[37] The same session of the legislature which authorized banks to subscribe to the government loan also directed the governor to pay immediately any direct tax levied by the national government during its recess. Neither of these bills aroused any opposition.[38]

In the following year (1813) the legislature authorized the governor to subscribe $1 million in the name of the state to the $16 million loan authorized in February. Governor Snyder delegated John Binns and David Acheson to raise the funds in Philadelphia. With little difficulty they raised the entire amount in a few months.[39] When the books on this loan were closed, it, too, was undersubscribed by more than $10 million. The government reopened the books in April and Stephen Girard, heading a consortium that included John Jacob Astor and David Parish, subscribed for the more than $10 million that had not been subscribed in the first offering. A third loan, for $7,500,000, offered in September 1813, was oversubscribed by more than $5 million, with banks and individuals in Pennsylvania again contributing generously.[40] The legislature also pledged all revenues from taxes on auction

[37] *Pennsylvania House Journal*, 1811-1812, pp. 430, 452-54, 718; *Pennsylvania Senate Journal*, 1811-1812, pp. 325, 376, 402-404; Pennsylvania *Gazette*, May 6, 1812; Stephen Girard Papers, Letters Received No. 464, American Philosophical Society, Philadelphia (1942), 29-55; Eyre to Roberts, May 2, 1812, Roberts Papers.

[38] *Pennsylvania Senate Journal*, 1811-1812, pp. 242-44, 478-515; *Pennsylvania House Journal*, 1811-1812, pp. 584, 593-94, 704-706.

[39] Snyder to Binns and Acheson, March 13, March 31, April 5, 1813, *Pennsylvania Archives*, 2d series, XII, 636, 637, 645. See also *Pennsylvania Archives*, 4th series, IV, 810-11, 829-30. For the legislation see *Pennsylvania House Journal*, 1812-1813, pp. 207-10, 214.

[40] *American State Papers: Finance*, II, 467. Kenneth L. Brown, "Stephen Girard's Bank," *Pennsylvania Magazine of History and Biography*, LXVI (January 1942), 29-55.

sales to the building of two ships of war to be given to the national government.[41]

The continued failure of American arms in 1813 aroused some resentment for the conduct of the war, but this resentment expressed itself not in demands for a cessation of hostilities, but in demands for more vigorous prosecution.[42] This attitude can best be seen in Republican reaction to the Czar's offer to mediate between the United States and Great Britain. The Pittsburgh *Mercury* approved of the American government's speedy acceptance of the offer, holding it up as another example of the administration's desire for an honorable peace. It warned, however, that the possibility of mediation should not lead to a diminution of the war effort. The British would not give up their "haughty pretension" until the United States proved itself in battle and the Czar's efforts could not produce a peace compatible with American honor until the nation's armies showed some success. The *Commonwealth* was much more cautious. Britain's earlier actions had proved she could not be trusted. "Peace concluded on honorable terms . . . is a consummation devoutly to be wished," but to begin negotiations without some assurances would only arouse the Federalists to "more ardent efforts to gain peace at any cost." The *Commonwealth* suggested that as the country undertook negotiations it should redouble its efforts in the field. Duane's sentiments were mixed. He first noted the offer without comment, gave cautious approval a few days later, but turned completely against the project when he learned that Gallatin was to be the chief negotiator.

In the Pennsylvania legislature the selection of two new senators to replace Gregg and Leib brought forth similar

41 *Pennsylvania House Journal*, 1812-1813, pp. 207-10, 214.
42 Philadelphia *Aurora*, March 8, March 9, March 11, April 6, April 8, April 14, May 13, 1813; Pittsburgh *Commonwealth*, Feb. 23, Feb. 24, Feb. 27, April 21, 1813.

sentiments. In February 1814, without holding a caucus, the Republican members of the legislature nominated and easily elected Jonathan Roberts to fill the vacancy created by Leib's resignation. There was little debate, but what comments were made stressed Roberts's loyalty to the administration, his support of the declaration of war, and his vigorous prosecution of it.[43]

In December 1812, the legislature had elected Abner Lacock to fill Gregg's seat. There was some opposition of his nomination and election, but none of it was based on his strong support for the administration and the war. The leader of the opposition was William J. Duane, son of the editor of the *Aurora*, and a leader of the anti-Snyder faction when he was a member. Duane received the support of Pittsburgh Republicans who still resented Lacock's victory over Tannehill in 1810.[44] Those sentiments indicate that despite the bleak military situation the people of Pennsylvania remained convinced of the wisdom of the war, and of the necessity to fight it to a military conclusion.

The prosperity which the war brought to Pennsylvania may account for its popular support. Pennsylvania farmers received good prices for their products and Pennsylvania suppliers found a good buyer in the armed forces, both state militia and federal troops. In November 1813, flour sold for $6.28 a hundredweight. Before the war a barrel of flour had brought only $10.24 (a barrel contains 196 pounds of flour). Potatoes sold for $0.75 per bushel;

[43] *Pennsylvania House Journal*, 1814-1815, pp. 21, 44-49; Pittsburgh *Commonwealth*, April 7, April 15, April 21, 1813; Pittsburgh *Mercury*, April 22, 1813; Philadelphia *Aurora*, April 3, April 7, April 9, April 15, April 16, April 17, 1813. For similar expressions see Washington *Reporter*, May 3, 1813, Carlisle *Gazette*, April 19, 1813.

[44] For a biographical sketch of Lacock see *Dictionary of American Biography*, X, 521-22. On Lacock's proadministration stand see Binns to Roberts, Nov. 13, 1812. On his election as senator see *Pennsylvania House Journal*, 1812-1813, pp. 40-41, 53-55.

hay brought $20 per ton. The letters in the Denny-O'Hara
collection indicate that the firm was doing an excellent
business supplying troops. Occasionally it had more
orders than it could fill.[45] This prosperity even affected
the Federalists. Rogers wrote Roberts that their defeat in
elections did not disturb the Federalists. "They do not
care about elections so long as flour is so much in demand."[46]

Manufacturing also made great strides. The Philadelphia papers contained numerous offers to sell domestically
manufactured goods, advertisements seeking skilled work-
men, and notices for the sale of lots suitable for factories.
The existence of a wartime boom was confirmed bitterly
by the Pennsylvania *Gazette*. "The War-Hawks are thriv-
ing and fattening upon the hard earnings of the industrial
and peaceable part of the community. Many who eighteen months since were starving . . . have become sleek
and fat."[47]

Whether because of the economic boom consequent
upon the outbreak of the war, or the continued conviction
that the national honor and the future of the Republican
party required the prosecution of the war to a successful
military conclusion, Pennsylvania Republicans gave the
war strong support and continued to back the administration of James Madison. Pennsylvania richly deserves to
be called "The Keystone in the Democratic Arch."

[45] Pittsburgh *Commonwealth*, Nov. 3, 1813, Jan. 4, Feb. 5, March 8,
1814; Arthur H. Cole, *Wholesale Commodity Prices in the United States
1700-1861* (Cambridge, 1938), 141.
[46] Rogers to Roberts, Nov. 1, 1812, Roberts Papers.
[47] Oct. 14, 1813.

Conclusion

The sixteen votes provided by Pennsylvania for the declaration of war constituted not only the largest vote in favor of war from any delegation in Congress, but the highest percentage of any of the large delegations. This overwhelming support for the declaration of war was not an isolated instance. From 1807 to 1812 Pennsylvania's Republican congressmen gave equally strong support to the administration's efforts to substitute economic coercion for war and strongly defended Jefferson's and then Madison's foreign policy. The editorials in the state's Republican press, the resolutions of the state's General Assembly, the speeches of the governor, and the results of congressional and presidential elections indicate that the people of Pennsylvania also approved of the policies of the national government and endorsed the position of their congressional delegation. When Congress finally did declare war the people of Pennsylvania supported the war effort as staunchly as they had supported the declaration of war and opposed every effort to end the war before a military victory had been won.

Pennsylvania's support cannot be explained by applying the western and economic causes associated with the work of Julius Pratt, George Rogers Taylor, and Margaret Latimer. The evidence shows that there was no land hunger in Pennsylvania, no desire to annex Canada, and, except as a continuation of a long-existing demand to annex Florida, no particularly new desire for that territory. Certainly there is no evidence to indicate that Pennsylvania participated in a sectional bargain with any area for the acquisition of territory. At best, Pennsylvanians supported the invasion of Canada and Florida for tactical reasons, hoping to use any victories there as negotiable items at the conference table. Neither is there any indication that Pennsylvanians were overly concerned about Indian depredations on the frontier. The evidence also shows that Pennsylvania did not suffer an economic depression in the prewar years. The commercial sector of the economy did, indeed, sustain serious losses because of the commercial policy of the national government, but on the whole such losses were temporary. Most commercial men successfully shifted their capital to other areas with profit to themselves and benefits to the community. Domestic manufacturing in Pennsylvania increased significantly during the period, and tremendous strides were taken in the development of internal improvements. This expansion provided a good area for capital investment and sufficient employment for those who would otherwise have become unemployed as a result of cessation of commerce. Meanwhile agricultural prices remained high and the revenues of the state increased annually.

The more recent research of such diplomatic historians as Bradford Perkins, Reginald Horsman, and Roger Brown offer a more plausible explanation. Britain's violations of American neutral rights hurt American pride much more deeply than they hurt the American pocketbook. A scanning of the newspapers and correspondence of the period strongly suggests that considerations of national honor contributed substantially to the formation of Pennsylvania attitudes. The constant reiteration of phrases such as "the independence of the nation must be maintained," "the people have honor and pride and are willing to defend them," and the many references to national honor occur too regularly to be taken lightly. References to British actions as "debasing," "degrading," and "insulting" indicate that the nation's pride was hurt. Particularly interesting is the constant conjunction on the words "honor" and "independence." There is no evidence to show that any Pennsylvanian actually feared that America's existence as an independent nation was really threatened in any political or physical sense. More accurately, the phrase "honor and independence" implies that a nation which allows its honor to be defiled and its flag to be disgraced, which does not actively defend its rights against usurpation and its ships against molestation, will never be considered as an equal power in world affairs either by the other nations of the world or by its own citizens. This idea was sometimes expressed in the more proselytical sense as the need to prove to a world of monarchs and tyrants that a republican government could defend its rights and protect its people. To those Pennsylvanians who viewed the Federalist minority not only as anti-Republican, but as antirepublican, the need to prove the ability of republican institutions was also a consideration. The evidence from Pennsylvania does not warrant the conclusion that the need to prove the viability of republicanism was a major cause of the war. However, it does warrant the addition of such considerations to the broader thesis that considerations of national honor did play an important role in developing war sentiment in Pennsylvania.

The hope, or belief, that the policy of commercial restriction would benefit the state economically by giving an impetus to domestic manufactures and the presumption that war would speed the process of economic development were also factors which determined the attitudes and actions of Pennsylvanians.

Partisan considerations help to explain Pennsylvania's strong support of the war and the Republican administration which declared and fought it. Since the "revolution" of 1800, Pennsylvania had, in fact, been the cornerstone of the Republican edifice. Within the state the party was intermittently torn by factional disputes, but it always united on national issues to support the policies of the Republican administration and to send Republicans to Congress. The votes of the Pennsylvania delegations to the Eleventh and Twelfth congresses show a great concern for party regularity and a remarkable record of support of administration measures.

In addition to the habit of party regularity, concern for the future success of the party also motivated many Pennsylvania politicians. Their correspondence reveals a concern at the revival of Federalist strength and agitation both in the state and in the nation. Many were convinced that the people had tired of the peaceful methods of the government and wished to settle the nation's international difficulties, one way or another, without further ado. They concluded that if the administration did not act quickly and decisively, the people would look elsewhere for leadership. To avert election losses they urged war.

The relative importance of any of these factors is impossible to assess. All necessary conditions, in the words of John Stuart Mill, are "equally indispensable." It is possible, however, to give primacy to one particular factor, and Britain's violations of American neutral rights must be accorded this position. Without impressment and the orders-in-council America's honor would not have been put to the test; the ascendancy of the Republican party would not have been threatened, the nation's economic dependence on Great Britain would not have been so obvious, and war would not have been necessary. As it was, Britain's maritime policy aroused a configuration of feelings, attitudes, and fears which only a war could satisfy.

Bibliographical Note

The footnotes to this study will guide the reader to the primary and secondary sources I have used in analyzing the development of attitudes toward Great Britain which finally prompted Pennsylvania Republicans to support a declaration of war. In this essay I hope to include only those materials which I found particularly useful or those not previously examined thoroughly by other historians.

The Historical Society of Pennsylvania in Philadelphia has the most extensive collection of sources concerning Pennsylvania history. The papers of Jonathan Roberts, Alexander J. Dallas, Charles J. Ingersoll, and William Jones provide the clearest insight into the changing attitudes of leading Pennsylvania politicians, while the Lea and Febiger Collection contains important information on economic conditions.

In Pittsburgh, the Western Pennsylvania Historical Society has numerous small collections, relatively unused by historians, dealing with business, industry, and, to a lesser extent, politics. The most useful are the Armour Collection and the Denny-O'Hara Papers. Other useful collections are the Isaac Craig Papers at the Carnegie Library in Pittsburgh, the Gregg Collection and Pennsylvania Miscellany at the Library of Congress and the Albert Gallatin Papers at the New York Historical Society in New York City. All these depositories haxe extensive newspaper files of small town Pennsylvania newspapers.

The state of Pennsylvania has been among the most successful in publishing its official documents. The second, fourth, and ninth series of the *Pennsylvania Archives* deal with the period covered in this work. *The Guide to the Pennsylvania Archives* published by the Pennsylvania Historical and Museum Commission is an indispensable aid to anyone using the *Pennsylvania Archives*.

The number of published works on the War of 1812 is a measure of the interest that the war has had for American historians. Warren H. Goodman summarized all that had been written to 1940 in "The Origins of the War of 1812: A Survey of Changing Interpretations" (*Mississippi Valley Historical Review*, XXVIII [September 1941]). Roger Brown, *The Republic in Peril* (New-York, Columbia University Press: 1964), Reginald Horsman, *The Causes of of the War of 1812* (Philadelphia, University of Pennsylvania Press: 1962), and Bradford Perkins, *Prologue to War* (Berkeley, University of California Press: 1961), are the most useful studies to have appeared since Goodman's summary was published.

The only full length study of Pennsylvania that covers this period is Sanford W. Higgenbotham, *The Keystone of the Democratic Arch, Pennsylvania Politics, 1800-1816* (Harrisburg, Pennsylvania Historical and Museum Commission: 1952). It is a goldmine of information but so awkwardly organized and poorly indexed that it is difficult to use. William H. Egle, *History of the Commonwealth of Pennsylvania* (Philadelphia, E. M. Gardner: 1883) and H. M. Jenkins, *Pennsylvania, Colonial and Federal* (Philadelphia, Historical Publishing House: 1903) are also useful. Not to be discounted as sources of information unavailable elsewhere are the various county histories cited in the notes. They vary in quality and reliability, and must be used carefully.

Index

143; approves Embargo of 1812,
149; demands vigorous prosecution of the war, 168
Crawford county: land available
in, 10
Crawford, William: votes against
Macon's Bill #2, 111; supports
war preparations, 137; condemns
lack of party unity, 138; shares
lodgings with Findley and Smilie,
139n; supports Madison in 1812,
176

Dallas, Alexander J.: works for
party unity, 179; mentioned, 110
Dauphin County: in elections of
1812, 181
Dauphin *Guardian*: condemns British intrigue among Indians, 12;
condemns attack on *Chesapeake*,
51; supports Embargo of 1807,
92; mentioned, 8
Davis, Roger: elected to 12th
Congress, 119
Delaware County: prosperity in,
35
Duane, William: condemns attack
on *Chesapeake*, 48; opposes negotiations with G. Rose, 56;
doubts sincerity of Erskine, 59;
condemns repudiation of Erskine
agreement, 60; condemns appointment of Jackson, 61; advocates war, 61, 78, 129, 136,
142, 167; approves negotiation
with Foster, 63, 64; asserts failure of economic coercion, 66; approves Embargo of 1807, 92, 93,
107, 123; condemns Macon's Bill
#2, 114; supports Madison, 116,
134, 176; condemns Federalist
opposition, 142; approves Embargo of 1812, 148; opposed to
Snyder in state politics, 159; hostile to Gallatin, 159; predicts
Madison victory in 1812, 180;
opposes Russian mediation, 191;
mentioned, 49, 57, 96, 169
Duane, William J.: son of William
Duane, 179; urges party unity,
179; opposes Lacock's election
to Senate, 192

Embargo of 1807: economic effect
of, 27, 29, 33, 40; failure of, 46,
63; as stimulus to manufacturing,
49, 88; as a protective measure,
54; an issue in election of 1808,
55; approved by McKean, 58;
approved by Pennsylvania legislature, 58; approved by Seybert,
72; as alternative to war, 90, 102,
104, 128; mentioned, 25, 26, 62,
83, 86, 160
Embargo of 1812: approved by
Aurora, 72; approved Carlisle
Gazette, 72; approved by Pennsylvania Republicans, 72; approved by Smilie, 72; mentioned,
28, 71, 128, 146
Erie County: land available in, 10;
seeks arms against Indians, 13
Erskine agreement: signed, 59, 60;
repudiated, 60
Erskine, David: British negotiator,
59, 62
Evans, James: approves attack on
Canada, 22; condemns appointment of Jackson, 60
Eyre, Manuel: describes prosperity,
40; supports war preparations,
70, 136; supports Embargo of
1812, 73, 150; advocates war,
142

Ferguson, Russel, 26
Findley, William: opposes annexation of Canada, 9, 15, 20; concerned about Indian menace, 13,
14; describes prosperity, 40; supports war preparations, 136, 137;
shares lodgings with Smilie and
Crawford, 139n; mentioned, 21,
91
Florida: desire for, 7, 8, 195; as
tactical objective, 23
Foster, Augustus: appointed British minister to U. S., 64
Fox, Edward: condemns "Henry
affair," 18; supports Embargo of
1812, 73, 149; complains of congressional slowness, 129; supports vigorous war effort, 168;
mentioned, 144
Fur trade, 19

Gallatin, Albert: opposition to, 145, 159; plans for war finance, 188; mentioned, 83, 122, 159

Gerry, Elbridge: vice presidential candidate in 1812, 168

Girard, Stephen: describes prosperity, 40; subscribes to war loan, 189, 190

Gloniger, John: elected to Congress in 1812, 181

Grayson, John: volunteers for militia, 76

Gregg, Andrew: opposes war, 21, 159, 161; introduces nonimportation bill of 1806, 47, 81; doubts sincerity of George Rose, 56; defeated for Senate, 91; condemns congressional indecision, 110; votes for war, 161; supports Madison in 1812, 176; mentioned, 53, 59, 63, 68, 83, 85, 104, 160

Harrisburg *Times:* condemns attack on *Chesapeake,* 51; opposes Embargo of 1807, 94

Harrison, George, 154

Hiester, Daniel: opposes annexation of Florida, 24; not a party regular, 91; votes against Macon's Bill #2, 111; defeated for Congress in 1811, 118

Hiester, Joseph, 91, 130

Henry, John: British spy, 18

"Henry Affair": campaign issue in 1812, 19

Higgins, Jesse: condemns attack on *Chesapeake,* 20; doubts sincerity of George Rose, 57; of David Erskine, 59; supports Embargo of 1807, 102, 103

Hoge, William: votes against Embargo of 1807, 86; mentioned, 90

Hollingsworth, Paschal, 150, 151

Horsman, Reginald, 54, 195

Hyneman, John: candidate for Congress in 1811, 133

Indians: British intrigue among, 6, 7, 11, 19

Ingersoll, Charles: opposes attacks

on Canada, 22; explains causes of war, 46; describes Philadelphia, 126; supports war effort, 167, 168; supports Madison in 1812, 175; mentioned, 17, 124

Ingersoll, Jared: opposition vice-presidential candidate in 1812, 174

Jackson, Francis James: appointed British minister to U. S., 60; appointment opposed, 62, 64.

Jarret, Henry: volunteers for militia, 76

Jefferson, Thomas, 14, 29, 94, 98, 106, 121, 125, 126, 194

Jenkins, Robert: opposes annexation of Florida, 24; approves exemptions to Embargo, 88; not a party regular, 91; votes against Macon's Bill #2, 111; defeated for Congress in 1811, 118, 131; mentioned, 105

Jones, William: supports Embargo of 1807, 54, 98; doubts sincerity of Rose, 57; doubts sincerity of Erskine, 59; advocates war, 67; opposes nonintercourse, 107; supports Embargo of 1812, 150; mentioned, 21, 53, 56, 79, 83, 104

Kelly, James: votes for nonimportation bill, 83; opposes exemptions to Embargo, 88; mentioned, 105

Kraus, John, 10, 35

Lacock, Abner: advocates war, 78; elected to Congress in 1811, 119, 132; shares lodgings with Roberts, 139n; hostile to Leib, 162; elected to Senate, 192

Lancaster County: congressional elections of 1811 in, 133; public meeting in opposes Madison, 174

Latimer, Margaret, 25, 194

Leech, Richard: advocates war, 67, 136; condemns congressional inactivity, 144

Lefever, Joseph: opposes annexation of Canada, 9; not reelected